6.75
2089

Mark as Story

MARK AS STORY

AN INTRODUCTION TO THE NARRATIVE
OF A GOSPEL

DAVID RHOADS
and
DONALD MICHIE

Foreword by Reynolds Price

FORTRESS PRESS • **PHILADELPHIA**

COPYRIGHT © 1982 BY FORTRESS PRESS

All rights reserved. No part of this publication may be reproduced, stored in a retrieval system, or transmitted in any form or by any means, electronic, mechanical, photocopying, recording, or otherwise, without the prior permission of the publisher.

Library of Congress Cataloging in Publication Data
Rhoads, David M.
  Mark as story.
  Includes bibliographical references.
  1. Bible. N.T. Mark—Criticism, interpretation,
    etc.
  I. Michie, Donald M. II. Title.
  BS2585.M53   226'.3066   81–43084
  ISBN 0–8006–1614–6   AACR2

9019L81   Printed in the United States of America   1–1614

Dedicated to our parents
Luke and Virginia Andrews Rhoads
and
Elmo and Maxie Orton Michie

Contents

Contents

Foreword

David Rhoads and Donald Michie have understandably denied themselves dubious assertions about the core of motive and purpose in Mark's little book. For contrast, I'll sever the guywires and—instructed by their patient examination and by my own long study of the baffling text—I'll dare a few claims and hope the reader tests them.

The Good News According to Mark has proved the most enduringly powerful narrative in the history of Western civilization, perhaps in the history of the world. As the oldest of the four Christian gospels, basic to the composition of at least two of the other gospels, it has exerted an enormous and continuous influence over Western thought and action since its birth somewhere between A.D. 65 and 70. (And if it has affected the West so profoundly, then it has unavoidably and sometimes disastrously affected the East.) It has thus succeeded on a literally unimaginable scale in the first aim of all narrative—the compulsion and maintenance of belief. The simplest tale—for example, a lost child restored to its mother through terror and danger—labors to compel our temporary belief in both an action and the demand of that action, in the events described and the need for a changed human conduct which those events imply.

Mark labors (and it is part of his charm and power that he labors visibly; he is not a born writer) to compel our belief that a Galilean named Jesus discovered himself in early manhood to be the Son of God, that his discovery was confirmed by mighty acts over the powers of evil and the forces of nature, but that he met with incomprehension from family and pupils, ultimately discovered a sacrificial destiny for himself, and advanced toward the spiritual nexus of his country to engage that destiny—killed in agony at the hands of uncomprehending strangers and apparently raised from death in invisible but eternal triumph.

Why does Mark wish us to attend and believe a story initially so incredible in detail and so repugnant in its picture of humankind? Because unlike most storytellers he believes his tale to be *necessary for life*—all human life in its significant eternal aspect. If we hear and believe the actual story—believe that the events so briskly described occurred in a particular time and place more or less as Mark describes them—then we can hardly avoid confronting the demand made by the events (the whole tale can be read aloud in little more than an hour). The demand is synonymous with the first words of Jesus reported by Mark—that we repent and put faith in the good news: the news that God has resumed control of history, the news that human life is no longer a dark bout of meaningless waste but is redeemed by boundless and permanent love. How a believer in Mark's tale is expected to behave in the remainder of his daily life is left bracingly but frighteningly to the believer's own deduction and invention.

In short Mark passionately wants us to believe his tale because he knows it to be true. How did he acquire such conviction? Rhoads and Michie do not speculate though in a note they mention the ancient tradition that a man named Mark was an associate of Jesus' chief pupil Simon Peter and that Mark commited himself to writing Peter's own memories of the words and actions of Jesus. That tradition is preserved in a brief passage from an otherwise lost work of Papias, Bishop of Hierapolis, in about A.D. 140. A translation of the relevant phrases of the Greek original might go thus:

> Mark, becoming Peter's interpreter, wrote down correctly all he remembered of the things said and done by the Lord though not in order; for he had neither heard the Lord nor followed him. . . .

That straightforward claim was recorded by Papias some seventy years after Peter's probably violent death in Rome and some hundred years after Jesus' own murder. There are numerous difficulties in the way of simple acceptance of so simple a claim; yet for reasons too complex to state here, I (and many other students) accept it. It is credible on its face, according as it does with our knowledge of the mechanics of human memory in history, and it explains both the uncomplicated surface and the internally convoluted originality of the work itself. No earlier literary document bears the slightest resemblance to Mark's. One man, overwhelmed by a second man's memories of a colossal third man, preserves these memories as an urgent legacy to our race.

Hordes of other men and women have preserved first- and secondhand memories in letters, diaries, poems, plays, novels, biographies. Why were Mark's memories—first- or secondhand—so successful in their purpose? His own answer might well have been "because the memories were so astounding in beauty and importance." We can be sure, however, that a vast majority of us would have been incapable of committing similar memories to such powerful form. The success of the gospel then lies in two huge resources—its subject matter (the secret truth it knows and struggles to reveal) and its strategies for revelation.

Rhoads and Michie have clarified more thoroughly than previous critics the strategies of architecture and language that are Mark's designs upon our hearts. I will not dilute their findings by summary. But I would like to point in conclusion to one overarching strategy upon which they do not elaborate and which seems to me to confirm the origin of the tale in a particularly personal historical memory.

Notice the degree to which Mark's gospel, in striking contrast with the other three, lays its narrative bet upon described *action* at the expense of conversation or monologue. Remember the often paralyzingly long halts for dialogue or sermon in Matthew, Luke, and John—those waits which make the boorishness of Jesus' pupils seem all the more credible. Then look at Mark's commitment to unflagging and clearly limned action. Jesus went here and did this; then he went there and did that; then the world did its will on him; then he did his last deed—he triumphed over death.

Human memory, especially memory more than a few hours old, is almost always the memory of action, gesture, scene. Speech is certainly not omitted or even slighted in Mark—though we may long to know what Jesus said about many things and though Mark seldom preserves short sayings of Jesus to match the plentiful staggering utterances of the gospel of John—but speech in Mark is almost always rendered as the direct result of prior action. Jesus is brought to an apparently dead girl; he says, "Little girl, I'm telling you, rise!" He is shown a child from the crowd; the child's body in his arms then evokes a long and interestingly connected meditation on human offense. Such a strategy could conceivably have resulted from conscious or even unconscious art. But for me, and for many of Mark's two millennia of readers, it is the surest validation of and signal toward the origin of his blazing immediacy—he reports, not invents, the good news: a thing that has happened and in sight of human eyes. The thing can recur each time the tale is read. Read and see.

REYNOLDS PRICE
Duke University

Preface

Five years ago I asked Don Michie, a friend from the Department of English, to show my students of New Testament Introduction how to read one of the gospels as one would read a short story. As I listened to this English teacher interpret the Gospel of Mark, I was fascinated by the fresh and exciting way in which he discussed the story. He talked about the suspense in the drama. He spoke of Jesus as a character struggling to get his message across. And he showed how the conflicts come to a climax in Jerusalem. The lecture left me more intrigued than ever with the Gospel of Mark. And the students became very much involved in subsequent discussions of the story.

Since that initial eye-opening experience, Don and I have spent much time working together on the Gospel of Mark. The interdisciplinary sharing we have done has stimulated both of us; and our respect for the author of this gospel as a fine storyteller has only increased with further study. Along the way we discovered other Markan scholars employing similar literary approaches, in particular many members of the Markan Seminar of the Society of Biblical Literature under the leadership of Werner Kelber. References in the footnotes to them and to their work do not adequately convey our indebtedness, nor do the footnotes adequately represent the rich variety of literary interpretations among Markan scholars. Our primary purpose in this book is to present our own interpretation, informed as it is by the work of others. Yet we hope that the footnotes will also lead other students of Mark's story to the interpretations of other scholars of Mark and that the book itself will stimulate further discussion.

We are indebted to so many people who helped in the process of writing the book—especially the students, colleagues, pastors, and lay people who have engaged us in discussion about Mark's gospel. We are grateful for grants from the American Philosophical Foundation and from Carthage College for bibliographical materials and travel. A generous grant from Siebert Lutheran Foundation of Milwaukee enabled us to take a leave of absence in the spring of 1978 in order to develop a book of study materials on the Gospel of Mark. Also, the support of our respective department chairpersons, Floyd Tolleson and Harold Kruger, has been crucial for the completion of the book. In addition, we are also appreciative of those who gave extensive reactions to the book at various stages: Thomas Boomershine, Joanna Dewey, Kim Dewey, Standish Henning, Wesley Kort, Sandy Roberts, Carol Smith, Mary Ann Tolbert, and Orval Wintermute. Others were helpful in the preparation of the translation: W. F. Stinespring, Clifford Dull, Trudy Kastens, James Wilde, and Larry Hurtado. Gladys Dart, Polly Haugland, Erna Williams, and Sue Witkauskis were excellent typists.

Especially we want to acknowledge the support of our families, Mary Alyce, Mike, and Amy Michie, Sandy Roberts, and Tania and Jessica Rhoads, without whose love and patience the completion of this project would have been impossible.

DAVID RHOADS
Carthage College

Introduction

When we enter the story world of the Gospel of Mark, we enter a world full of conflict and suspense, a world of surprising reversals and strange ironies, a world of riddles and hidden meanings. The hero of the story—perhaps the most memorable in all of literature—is most surprising of all.

The Gospel of Mark deals with the great issues—life and death, good and evil, human triumph and human failure. It is not a simple story in which virtue easily triumphs over vice, nor is it a collection of moralizations on life. What may on a cursory reading appear to be simple answers to many of life's complications are really very tough pronouncements fraught with irony and paradox: to be most important, one must be least; to enter the rule of God, one must become like a little child; nothing is hidden except to become known; whoever wants to save one's life must lose it.

Within the narrative itself many characters think they have an understanding of their situations only to discover that what they had expected is suddenly overturned: the disciples follow Jesus expecting glory and recognition only to find servitude and death confronting them; the authorities kill Jesus in order to preserve their traditions and authority, but they doom themselves by their action; the women come to anoint the dead Jesus, but discover he is among the living.

Not only is this story full of intrigue, but the writer has told the story in such a way as to have certain effects on the reader. The reader experiences much the same in bafflement and reversals as do the characters. The author has used sophisticated literary techniques, developed the characters and the conflicts, and built suspense with deliberateness, telling the story in such a way as to generate certain emotions and insights in the reader. The ending especially has a surprising twist and leads the reader to rethink much of the drama. Thus, analyzing the narrative involves understanding not only the world of the story but also the impact which it may have on the reader.

In our culture we seldom experience the total impact of Mark's gospel because we seldom hear or read the story in its entirety. We usually encounter Mark's gospel in bits and pieces. We often hear verses quoted outside the context of the whole story, or we hear individual episodes read at worship. Such an experience of Mark's story is similar to hearing quotations from different Shakespearean plays without ever having read or seen one of those plays in its entirety. This fragmentation is reinforced by the division of the gospel into chapters and verses which, though common gospel translation, was not part of the original construct. Some translations further break up the text by headlining each episode. In addition, many of the modern methodologies for studying Mark's gospel have differentiated the sources from the author's editorial additions and the traditions from the author's arrangement of them. As necessary as these methods are to investigate the history and to understand the author's intentions, they do not help us see this gospel as a unified narrative.

How often have we heard Mark's story as a dramatic presentation or reading? How many of us have even read it alone at one sitting? Perhaps those in the first century who first heard the Gospel of Mark read aloud to them on a single occasion were best able to participate in the drama of the story, experience the tension of the conflicts, identify with the characters, feel the suspense about the outcome, and see the story world as the narrator of the story shows it.[1] Emerging from the story world, they were perhaps also able to see and act in the world in new ways. Likewise, the contemporary reader benefits from a work of literature by entering the world of the individual work and thereby through imagination experiencing different aspects of life and seeing the world in new ways.

The purpose of this book is to aid in recovering the experience of the Gospel of Mark as unified narrative, to better understand the story as a whole and to appreciate its impact.[2] To do this we have drawn extensively on the work of contemporary literary criticism.[3] Literary critics have developed methods to analyze the formal features of narrative, such as the role of the narrator, point of view, style, plot, settings, and characters. Although these methods were developed primarily in the study of modern novels and short stories, most ancient narratives share the same formal features, and the use of these methods greatly aids students in their study of ancient literature such as the Gospel of Mark.

Introduction

We have also drawn upon the recent work of biblical scholars who use literary categories to interpret Mark's narrative.[4]

The study of narrative emphasizes the unity of the final text.[5] Such a study of the formal features of Mark's gospel tends to reveal the narrative as whole cloth. The narrator's point of view in telling the story is consistent throughout.[6] The plot is coherent: events that are anticipated come to pass; conflicts are resolved; predictions are fulfilled.[7] The characters are consistent from one scene to the next, fulfilling the roles they take on and the tasks they adopt.[8] Literary techniques of storytelling, along with elements of style and organization, unify the narrative at many levels: phrase, sentence, episode, and structure. There is also a consistent depiction of the human condition, sin, faith, God's rule, ethical choices, and the possibilities for human change. Thus, the unity of the gospel is apparent in the remarkable integrity of the story it tells.[9] Although scholars know little about the origin of this gospel,[10] a literary study of its formal features suggests that the author succeeded in creating a unified narrative.

Once the unity of the story is experienced, one is able to participate in the world of the story. Although the author of the Gospel of Mark certainly used sources rooted in the historical events surrounding the life of Jesus, the final text is a literary creation with an autonomous integrity,[11] just as Leonardo's portrait of the Mona Lisa exists independently as a vision of life apart from a resemblance or nonresemblance to the person who posed for it or as a play of Shakespeare has integrity apart from reference to the historical characters depicted there. One can read and interpret Mark's gospel as a story independent from the real people and events upon which it is based. The author of the gospel has not simply collected traditions, organized them, made connections between them, and added summaries, but has also told a story—a dramatic story—with characters whose lives we follow to the various places they travel and through the events in which they are absorbed.

Mark's story is complete in itself not only apart from reference to the historical events on which it is based but also apart from the other gospels, which are also autonomous stories about Jesus. In narrative study, we cannot legitimately use the other gospels to "fill out" or to "fill in" some unclear passage in Mark's story. Rather we need to read Mark's gospel more carefully as a self-sufficient story. To interpret

3

Mark's gospel in its autonomous integrity we bracket what other sources or later generations have said or believed about Jesus.

None of these considerations means that our general knowledge of the first century is not helpful in the interpretation of the story; indeed, it is often crucial. But using general knowledge of the times is a different matter from using sources or information which "add" to the story.

Thus, Mark's narrative contains a closed and self-sufficient world with its own integrity, its own imaginative past and future, its own sets of values, and its own universe of meanings.[12] When viewed as a literary achievement the statements in Mark's narrative, rather than being a representation of historical events, refer to the people, places, and events *in the story*.[13] The feeding of five thousand people in a desert is a dramatic episode in the continuum of Mark's *story,* a miraculous feeding with a conflict between the teacher and his disciples, every detail vivid and relevant. Jesus, Herod, and the centurion are dramatic *characters*. The exorcisms, the journeys, the trial and execution are *events* in the narrative world, each element important and integral. The desert, Capernaum, and Jerusalem are *settings* highly charged with meaning in the world of the story. It is this story world which the reader enters. And this story world, along with its presentation in the narrative, is the subject of our study. *Unless otherwise identified as helpful historical information from the culture of the first century, all subsequent discussion about people, places, and events deals only with the story world of Mark's gospel.*

Many literary critics distinguish between the content of a narrative, its *story,* and the form of a narrative, its *rhetoric.* The story refers to "what" a narrative is about—the basic elements of the narrative world—events, characters, and settings. Rhetoric refers to "how" that story is told in a given narrative in order to achieve certain effects upon the reader. Thus we can distinguish between "what" the story is about and "how" the story is told.[14] The "what" and the "how," story and rhetoric, content and form are obviously inseparable in narrative, and their interrelation is integral to the impact of a narrative. Only for purposes of analysis do we isolate a feature of narrative, such as character or style, and then only to interpret it in light of the whole narrative. But this fragmentary analysis never replaces the unitary impact of the narrative itself.[15]

4

Introduction

We begin our study with the gospel itself, a fresh translation laid out like a short story with no chapter or verse designations. The translation reflects the integrity of the story as a whole, including narrative patterns and literary techniques, and takes into account elements of the narrative such as plot line, character development, verbal motifs, and suspense.

Our study then proceeds to an analysis of Mark's narrative along the lines of inquiry provided by contemporary literary criticism. In Chapter 2 we will look at rhetoric, or "how" the author of the Gospel of Mark presents this story in the narrative: the role of the narrator, point of view, standards of judgment, style, narrative patterns, and other rhetorical devices. Then in subsequent chapters, we will explore the story, or "what" the narrative is about. In chapter 3 we will discuss the settings as a dynamic context for the action of this story. In chapter 4 we will focus on events of the plot, primarily on the conflicts which Jesus has with demons, with the authorities, and with his disciples. And in Chapter 5 we will evaluate the characters: Jesus, the authorities, the disciples, and the minor characters. The three chapters about setting, plot, and character are informed by the earlier analysis of the rhetoric of Mark's gospel.

In the final chapter, we will highlight the themes of the story and focus on the total impact the narrative may have on readers, ancient and modern.

1

The Gospel of Mark

INTRODUCTION TO THE TRANSLATION

The translation which follows is set out like a short story so that the reader may experience the story as a whole.[1] There are no chapter or verse designations. The paragraph divisions usually mark a shift in scenes, a change of speaker, or the conclusion of a conflict, all intended to highlight the dialogue, action, and movement of the story. Punctuation is often chosen to establish connections in the narrative or to bring out the drama of the action.[2] Generally, we have followed a standard Greek text and have translated it so as to bring out the drama of the story, as we see it, in the original.[3]

Every translation is limited in adequately representing the original language, and every translation is an interpretation. Yet each translation strives to be as close to the meanings of the original as possible. We have tried to find single words or brief phrases which most faithfully render the Greek words, employing everyday language without softening the strangeness or harshness of Mark's choice of words. Often, we have chosen fresh words which convey meanings and nuances not always highlighted: "pardon of sins," "rule of God," "riddles," and so on. Also, we have tried to select a vocabulary that is appropriate to the atmosphere, character traits, conflicts, emotions, and plot development in the world of the story. In addition, our choice of words takes into account the context of the whole story. Many translators determine meaning primarily from the immediate episodic context, thus translating the same recurring Greek word differently in each episode. For example, the Greek word *hodos* has been variously rendered "way," "journey," "path," and "road" in different contexts of the same translation. Similarly, *paradidomi* has been variously translated as "arrested," "handed over," "delivered up," and "betrayed" throughout the same translation. By contrast, we have tried to translate the same Greek word with the same English word throughout the story, so that the reader can see the verbal motifs of "the way" and "handed

6

over" recurring, as they do in the Greek, throughout the story. We have consistently followed this procedure with verbal motifs, except in a few cases where the meaning would be distorted in a particular context.[4]

Also, we have tried to reflect many elements of the Markan style, even when it is somewhat awkward.[5] We have attempted in general to be faithful to the word order, the frequent use of participles, the various functions of the imperfect tense, the emphatic pronouns (usually in italics), emphatic negatives, and formulaic phrases.[6] We have also tried to reflect rhetorical devices such as the two-step progression, repetition, concentric structure, the asides of the narrator, and so on, which we will discuss later. These rhetorical devices contribute to the suspense and drama of the story.

We have faced a dilemma about gender in the translation and have reluctantly decided to translate consistently the masculine gender of the original Greek. Thus, for example, we use a masculine pronoun in reference to the masculine *theos* (God) and we translate the masculine *anthropos* in the singular and plural as "man" and "men." We also render accurately the masculine pronouns. We have done this in part to remain consistent in our attempt to be faithful to the original text and in part to retain specific plays on words, such as the play on words between "man" and "the son of man." In subsequent chapters we include masculine-gender language only where we quote the translation or allude to passages of the gospel, as, for example, in the phrases "the things of men" and "authority from men."

This translation is meant for use with this book. We encourage the reader to read the whole story at one sitting and to reread it with the subsequent chapters, each time looking for a different aspect of the rhetoric or the story world. We also encourage the reader to listen to the story read aloud, for hearing the story may help to broaden and deepen the experience of it.

THE GOSPEL OF MARK

The beginning of the good news about Jesus the anointed one, the son of God—just as it is written in Isaiah the prophet,
"Look, I am sending my messenger ahead of you,
who will pave your way,
a cry of one shouting in the desert,
'Prepare the lord's way,
make his paths level.' "

It was John baptizing in the desert and proclaiming a baptism of repentance for pardon of sins. And the whole Judean countryside and all the Jerusalemites were going out to him and were being baptized by him in the Jordan River, acknowledging their sins.

And John was wearing camel's hair with a leather band around his waist and was eating grasshoppers and wild honey. And he was proclaiming, saying, "After me is coming one stronger than I, the strap of whose sandals I'm not worthy to stoop and untie. *I* baptized you with water, but *he* will baptize you in the holy spirit."

And it happened in those days that Jesus came from Nazareth of Galilee and was baptized in the Jordan by John. Immediately coming up from the water he saw the heavens being ripped open and the spirit like a dove coming down onto him. And there was a voice from the heavens, "You are my only son. In you I took delight."

Immediately the spirit drove him out to the desert and he was in the desert forty days being tested by Satan. And he was among the wild animals, and the angels were serving him.

Now after John was handed over, Jesus came into Galilee proclaiming the good news about God, and saying, "The right time is fulfilled, and the rule of God has come near. Repent and put faith in the good news."

And passing along by the Sea of Galilee, he saw Simon and Andrew the brother of Simon casting nets in the sea, for they were fishermen.

Jesus said to them, "Come after me and I'll make you become fishers for men." And immediately leaving the nets, they followed him.

And going ahead a little further, he saw James the son of Zebedee and John his brother who were in the boat preparing the nets.

And immediately he called them. And leaving their father Zebedee in the boat with the hired hands, they went off after him.

They entered into Capernaum. And immediately on the Sabbath he entered into the synagogue and began teaching. And people were astounded at his teaching, for he was teaching them as one having authority and not like the legal experts.

Immediately a man with an unclean spirit was in their synagogue. It screamed out, saying, "What do you have against us, Jesus Nazarene? Did you come to destroy us? I know who you are—the holy one of God."

And Jesus rebuked it, saying, "Shut up and come out from him!" And the unclean spirit, convulsing the man and crying out in a loud cry, came out from him.

And everyone was so astonished that they were arguing among themselves, saying, "What is this? A new teaching with authority? He gives orders even to the unclean spirits and they obey him!" And the report about him immediately went out everywhere, into the whole surrounding countryside of Galilee.

Immediately coming out from the synagogue they went with James and John into the house of Simon and Andrew. Now Simon's mother-in-law was lying down, with a fever, and immediately they told him about her. And approaching her, he grasped her hand and raised her up. And the fever left her and she began serving them.

Now when it was evening, after the sun set, people were bringing to him all those who were sick and those possessed by demons. The whole city was gathered at the door. And he healed many who were sick with various diseases and drove out many demons. And he would not let the demons talk, because they knew him.

And early in the morning, while it was still quite dark, rising he came out and went off to a desert place and there was praying. And Simon and those with him tracked him down, and they found him and said to him, "Everyone's seeking you."

And he said to them, "Let's go elsewhere, to the nearby towns, so I might proclaim there too, for that's why I came out." And he went proclaiming in their synagogues, in all Galilee, and driving out the demons.

A leper came to him, pleading with him, falling on his knees and saying to him, "If you want to, you're able to make me clean."

And moved by compassion, Jesus stretched out his hand and touched him, then said to him, "I want to. Be clean." And immediately the leprosy went away from him, and he was made clean.

And becoming harsh with him, immediately Jesus drove him out and said to him, "See that you say nothing at all to anyone, but go show yourself to the priest and make for your cleansing the offering Moses prescribed, as testimony to them."

But going out he began to proclaim freely and to spread the word around so that no longer was Jesus able to enter openly into a city, but was outside, in desert places. And people kept coming to him from everywhere.

When he entered again into Capernaum after some days, it was reported that he was in his house. And so many people gathered that there was no longer room, not even places at the door. And he was telling them the word.

And people came bringing to him a cripple carried by four of them. And not being able to get to him because of the crowd, they unroofed the roofing where he was, and digging through, they let down the mat on which the cripple was lying. And seeing their faith, Jesus said to the cripple, "Child, your sins are pardoned."

Now some of the legal experts were sitting there and thinking in their minds, "Why does this man talk like this? He blasphemes! Who is able to pardon sins except the one God?"

And immediately aware in his spirit that they were thinking like this within themselves, Jesus said to them, "Why are you thinking these things in your minds? Which is easier, to say to the cripple 'Your sins are pardoned' or to say 'Rise and take up your mat and walk'? But so you may know that the son of man has authority to pardon sins on the earth"—he said to the cripple—"I'm telling you, rise, take up your mat, and go off to your house."

And he rose and immediately taking up the mat he went out in front of everyone, with the result that everyone was stunned and glorified God, saying, "We never saw anything like this."

He went out again by the sea. And the whole crowd came to him, and he was teaching them. And passing by, he saw Levi the son of Alphaeus sitting at the toll-tax office, and he said to him, "Follow me." And rising he followed him.

And it happened that he was reclining to eat in his house. And many toll collectors and sinners were reclining to eat with Jesus and his disciples, for there were many and they were following him.

And when the legal experts of the Pharisees saw that he was eating with the sinners and toll collectors, they said to his disciples, "Why is he eating with the toll collectors and sinners?"

And hearing it, Jesus said to them, "Those who are healthy have no need for a doctor, but those who are sick do. I came not to call righteous people, but sinners."

John's disciples and the Pharisees were fasting. And people came and said to him, "Why are the disciples of John and the disciples of the Pharisees fasting, but your disciples aren't fasting?"

And Jesus said to them, "Are the attendants of the bridegroom able to fast while the bridegroom is with them? As long as they have the bridegroom with them, they aren't able to fast. But the days will come when the bridegroom is taken away from them, and then they will fast in that day.

"No one sews a patch of unshrunk cloth on an old cloak. Otherwise the patch pulls away from it, the new from the old, and the rip becomes worse. And no one puts fresh wine into old wineskins. Otherwise the wine will burst the wineskins, and the wine is destroyed with the wineskins. Instead, put fresh wine into new wineskins."

It happened that on the Sabbath he was going along through the grain fields, and his disciples began to make their way, picking the heads of the grain. And the Pharisees said to him, "Look, why are they doing what is not legal on the Sabbath?"

And he said to them, "Haven't you ever read what David did when he had a need, and he and those with him were hungry? How he entered into the house of God when Abiathar was High Priest and ate the bread of the presence, which it's not legal for anyone to eat except the priests, and he also gave to those who were with him?"

And he said to them, "The Sabbath originated for man, not man for the Sabbath. So, the son of man is lord even of the Sabbath."

He entered again into the synagogue, and a man was there who had a withered hand. And they were watching Jesus closely whether on the Sabbath he would heal him, so they might bring charges against him.

And he said to the man who had the withered hand, "Rise to the center!"

And Jesus said to them, "Is it legal on the Sabbath to do good or to do harm? To restore a life or to put to death?" But they kept quiet.

And looking around at them with anger, saddened by the hardening of their minds, he said to the man, "Stretch out the hand." And he stretched it out, and his hand was made new. And going out, the Pharisees immediately held council with the Herodians against him, how they might destroy him. Jesus withdrew with his disciples to the sea. And a huge number from Galilee followed, and also from Judea and from Jerusalem and from Idumea and across the Jordan and around Tyre and Sidon, a huge number, hearing what he was doing, came to him.

And he told his disciples to keep a little boat waiting for him because of the crowd, so they would not press him. For he healed so many that those having ailments were falling on him in order to touch him.

And the unclean spirits, when they saw him, would fall down before him and scream, saying, "You are the son of God." And he would rebuke them vehemently not to make him known.

He went up onto the mountain and summoned those he wanted, and they went off to him. And he made twelve so they might be with him and he might send them out to proclaim and to have authority to drive out the demons.

And he made the twelve—and Simon he nicknamed "Peter," and James the son of Zebedee and John the brother of James he nicknamed "Boanerges" which means "Sons of Thunder," also Andrew and Philip and Bartholomew and Matthew and Thomas and James the son of Alphaeus and Thaddeus and Simon the Cananaean and Judas Iscariot who also handed him over.

He came into a house, and such a crowd came together again that they were not even able to eat bread. And when his family heard, they came out to seize him, for they were saying, "He's out of his mind."

And the legal experts who came down from Jerusalem were saying, "He's possessed by Beelzebul" and "By the ruler of the demons he drives out the demons."

And summoning them he began talking to them in riddles: "How is Satan able to drive out Satan? If a rule is divided against itself, that rule is not able to stand. And if a house is divided against itself, that house will not be able to stand. And if Satan did rise up against himself and was divided, he isn't able to stand but is at an end.

"On the other hand, surely no one is able to enter into the house of the strong one and plunder his goods, unless first he bind the strong one, and then he will plunder his house.

"I swear to you that everything will be pardoned the sons of men, their sins and whatever blasphemies they blaspheme. Yet whoever blasphemes against the holy spirit won't obtain a pardon ever, but is guilty of an eternal sin"—because they had been saying, "He has an unclean spirit."

His mother and his brothers came, and standing outside they sent someone to him, calling for him. A crowd was sitting around him, and they said to him, "Look, your mother and your brothers outside are seeking you."

And answering them, he said, "Who are my mother and my brothers?"

And looking around at those about him seated in a circle, he said, "Look, here are my mother and my brothers. For whoever does the will of God, *that* is my brother and sister and mother."

Again he began to teach by the sea. And such a very huge crowd gathered about him that he climbed into a boat and sat out on the sea. And the whole crowd was by the sea, on the land. And he was teaching many things in riddles and was saying to them in his teaching, "Hear! Look! The sower came out to sow. And it happened in the sowing that some fell beside the way, and the birds came and ate it up. Other seed fell on the rocky ground where there wasn't much soil, and immediately it sprouted up because the soil had no depth. And when the sun rose up, it was scorched, and because it had no root, it was withered. Other seed fell among the thorns, and the thorns came up and strangled it, and it didn't yield fruit. Other seed fell onto the good soil, and it yielded fruit, coming up and growing, and it produced thirty and sixty and a hundred per measure!" And he said, "Whoever has ears to hear, let him hear!"

When he was by himself, those about him with the twelve were asking him about the riddles. And he said to them, "To you has been given the mystery of the rule of God, but to those outside everything comes in riddles, so that

> looking they look,
> and don't see,
> and hearing they hear,
> and don't understand.

Otherwise they might turn around and be pardoned."

And he said to them, "Don't you know this riddle? And how will you learn all the riddles?

"The sower sows the word. Now there are those beside the way where the word is sown, and when they hear, immediately Satan comes and takes away the word which was sown in them. And there are those sown on the rocky places who when they hear the word immediately with joy receive it. Yet they don't have root in themselves but are short-lived. When oppression or persecution comes because of the word, immediately they stumble. And others are those sown among the thorns. Those are the ones who have heard the word, and the anxieties of the age and the lure of wealth and the desires for other things come in and strangle the word, and it is unfruitful. And there are these sown on the good soil, the ones who hear the word and receive it and produce fruit, thirty and sixty and a hundred per measure!"

And he said to them, "Is the lamp brought in to be put under the measuring basket or under the bed? Isn't it to be put on the lampstand? For nothing is hidden except to be made known, nor is anything secret but to come into the open. If anyone has ears to hear, let him hear!"

And he said to them, "Look at what you hear. By whatever measure you measure out, it will be measured out to you and increased for you. For whoever has, more will be given him. And whoever does not have, even what he has will be taken from him."

He said, "The rule of God is like this: a man throws the seed on the ground, then sleeps and rises, night and day, and the seed sprouts and lengthens—he doesn't know how. On its own, the earth produces fruit: first a stalk, then a head, then ripe grain in the head. Now when the fruit delivers up its yield, immediately he sends out the sickle because the harvest stands ready."

He said, "How shall we compare the rule of God? Or into what riddle shall we put it? It's like a grain of mustard, which when sown on the ground is smallest of all the seeds on the earth. And when it is sown it comes up and becomes the largest of all the shrubs and makes such great branches that the birds of heaven are able to nest in its shade."

And with many such riddles he was telling them the word, as they were able to hear it. Now he was not talking to them without a riddle, but privately for his own disciples he would unravel everything.

And he said to them on that day, when evening came, "Let's go over to the other side." And leaving the crowd, they took him along as he was, in the boat, and other boats were with him.

And a fierce squall of wind came, and the waves were dashing up into the boat, so that already the boat was filling. And Jesus was in the stern, on the boat cushion, sleeping. And they roused him, and said to him, "Teacher, don't you care that we're being destroyed?"

And waking up, he rebuked the wind and said to the sea, "Be quiet! Shut up!" And the wind quit, and there was a great calm.

And he said to them, "Why are you cowards? Don't you have faith yet?"

And they were frightened with great fear and were saying to each other, "So who is this that even the wind and the sea obey him?"

They came to the other side of the sea, to the district of the Gerasenes. As Jesus was getting out of the boat, immediately he was met from the graves by a man with an unclean spirit who had his dwelling among the graves. And no one was able to bind him any longer, not even with a chain, because he had been bound often with shackles and chains, but the chains had been shattered by him and the shackles smashed, and no one was strong enough to overpower him. And throughout every night and day, among the graves and in the mountains, he would scream and slash himself with stones.

But seeing Jesus from a distance, he ran and gave him obeisance, and screaming in a loud voice, he said, "What do you have against me, Jesus, son of the most high God? I'm putting you on oath, by God, not to torment me." For Jesus had been saying to him, "Unclean spirit, come out from the man!"

Jesus asked him, "What's your name?"

And he said to him, "My name is Legion, because we are many." And he pleaded with him wildly not to send them outside the district.

Now there at the side of the mountain a large herd of pigs was feeding. And the unclean spirits pleaded with him, saying, "Send us to the pigs so we might enter into them." And he let them do it.

And coming out, the unclean spirits entered into the pigs, and the herd—about two thousand—rushed down the bank into the sea and drowned in the sea.

And those who had been feeding the pigs fled and reported it in the city and in the fields. And people came to see what it was that had happened. And they came to Jesus and observed the demoniac, the one who had had the "Legion," sitting dressed and sane, and they were frightened. And those who saw it recounted for them how it happened to the demoniac and about the pigs. And they began to plead with Jesus to go off from their territory.

As Jesus was climbing into the boat, the demoniac began pleading with him that he might be with him. And Jesus did not let him, but instead said to him, "Go off to your house, to your family, and report to them what the Lord has done for you and how he showed you mercy." But he went away and began to proclaim in the Ten Cities what Jesus did for him, and everyone was amazed.

When Jesus had crossed over in the boat back to the other side, a huge crowd gathered about him, and he was by the sea.

And one of the synagogue rulers came, Jairus by name. And seeing Jesus, he fell at his feet and pleaded with him urgently, saying, "My little daughter is almost dead. Come lay hands on her so she might be restored and live." And Jesus went off with him, and a huge crowd was following him and pressing him.

There was a woman who had a flow of blood over the course of twelve years and had suffered greatly under many doctors and spent everything she had and not been helped, but rather was getting worse. Hearing about Jesus, she came in the crowd from behind and touched his cloak, for she had been saying, "If I touch just his clothes, I'll be restored." And immediately the source of her bleeding withered up, and she knew in her body that she was cured of the ailment.

And Jesus, immediately aware in himself of the power that had gone out from him, turned around in the crowd and said, "Who touched my clothes?"

And his disciples said to him, "You're looking at the crowd pressing against you, and you say 'Who touched me?'?" And Jesus kept looking around to see the one who had done this.

Now the woman, frightened and trembling, having realized what had happened to her, came and fell before him and told him the whole truth. He said to her, "Daughter, your faith has restored you. Go off in peace and be free of your ailment."

While he was still talking, people came from the home of the synagogue ruler, saying, "Your daughter died. Why still bother the teacher?"

But Jesus, overhearing the word spoken, said to the synagogue ruler, "Don't be afraid. Only have faith." And he did not let anyone at all follow along with him except Peter and James and John the brother of James.

And they came to the house of the synagogue ruler, and Jesus observed a disturbance, with sobbing and loud wailing. And entering he said to them,

"Why are you making a disturbance and sobbing? The little child didn't die, but is sleeping." And they jeered him.

But driving everyone out, he took along the father of the little child with the mother and those with him and went in where the little child was. And grasping the hand of the little child, he said to her, *"Talitha cumi,"* which is translated "Little girl, I'm telling you, rise!"

Immediately the little girl rose and began walking (for she was twelve-years-old). And they were stunned immediately with great astonishment. And he ordered them strictly to let no one know about this, then told them to give her something to eat.

He came out from there and went to his hometown, and his disciples followed him. And when Sabbath came he began to teach in the synagogue.

And many who heard were astounded, saying, "Where did this one get these things?" and "What is the wisdom given to this one that even works of power such as these come about through his hands? Isn't this the carpenter, Mary's son and a brother of James and Joses and Judas and Simon? And aren't his sisters here among us?" And he was a stumbling block to them.

And Jesus said to them, "A prophet doesn't lack honor except in his hometown and among his relatives and in his house." And he was not able there to do even one work of power, except that laying his hands on a few frail people he healed them. And he was amazed at their lack of faith.

He began going about the surrounding villages teaching. And he summoned the twelve and began to send them two by two and was giving them authority over the unclean spirits. And he was giving them orders to take nothing on the way except a walking stick only—no bread, no beggar's bag, no coins in the belt, but to strap on sandals and not wear two tunics.

And he said to them, "Wherever you enter into a house, stay there until you come out from that locale, and whatever place doesn't receive you or hear you, go out from there and shake off the dust under your feet as testimony against them." And going out, they proclaimed that people should repent. And they were driving out many demons and anointing with oil many frail people and healing them.

King Herod heard, for Jesus' name was becoming known and people were saying, "John the baptizer has been raised from the dead, and that's why the works of power are working in him." Others were saying, "He's Elijah." Others were saying, "He's a prophet like one of the prophets." But when Herod heard, he said, "The one I beheaded, John, he was raised."

For Herod himself had sent out and seized John and bound him in prison on account of Herodias, the wife of Philip his brother, because Herod married her. For John had been saying to Herod, "It's not legal for you to have the wife of your brother."

Now Herodias was holding a grudge against him and wanted to put him to death, but she wasn't able to, for Herod was afraid of John, knowing him to be a just and holy man, and was protecting him. And when he heard him, he was quite puzzled, but he was glad to hear him.

And an opportune day came when Herod on his birthday held a banquet for his greatest men and the military officers and the most important men of Galilee. When Herodias's own daughter entered and danced, she pleased Herod and those reclining to eat with him. The king said to the little girl, "Ask of me whatever you want, and I'll give it to you." And he swore an oath to her, "Whatever you ask of me, I'll give you, up to half of my kingdom."

And she went out and said to her mother, "What should I ask for?"

She said, "The head of John the baptizer."

And entering immediately with haste before the king, she asked, saying, "I want you right now to give me on a plate the head of John the Baptist."

The king became profoundly sad, but because of the oaths and those reclining to eat, he did not want to refuse her. And immediately sending for an executioner, the king ordered him to bring John's head.

And going off, he beheaded him in the prison and brought his head on a plate, then gave it to the little girl, and the little girl gave it to her mother.

And when his disciples heard, they came and took his corpse and put it in a grave.

Those sent out gathered around Jesus and reported to him all that they had done and taught. And he said to them, "You yourselves come privately to a desert place and rest a little." For many were coming and going, and they were not even having an opportunity to eat. And they went off in the boat to a desert place privately.

And many people saw them going and recognized them, and on foot from all the cities they ran together there and arrived ahead of them. And getting out Jesus saw a huge crowd, and he had compassion for them because they were like sheep without a shepherd, and he began to teach them many things.

Since by now the hour was getting late, his disciples approached him and said, "The place is a desert, and the hour is already late. Disband them, so they might go off to the surrounding fields and villages and buy themselves something to eat."

Answering, he said to them, "*You* give them something to eat."

And they said to him, "Surely we're not to go off and buy two hundred denarii worth of bread and give it to them to eat?"

He said to them, "How many loaves have you? Go see."

And finding out, they said, "Five, and two fish."

And he ordered them to have everyone recline group by group on the green grass. And they reclined to eat by companies of a hundred and of fifty.

And taking the five loaves and the two fish, looking up to heaven he blessed them, then broke the loaves apart and gave them to his disciples to set before them, and the two fish he distributed to everyone. And everyone ate and was satisfied.

And they took up twelve baskets full of scraps and leftover fish. And there were five thousand men who ate.

Immediately he compelled his disciples to climb into the boat and go ahead to the other side, to Bethsaida, while he himself disbanded the crowd. And taking leave of them, he went off to the mountain to pray.

When evening came, the boat was in the middle of the sea, and he was alone on the land. And seeing them straining in the rowing, for the wind was against them, about the fourth watch of the night he went towards them, walking on the sea.

And he wanted to go past them. But those who saw him walking on the sea thought he was a ghost and screamed out, for they all saw him and were terrified. Immediately he spoke to them and said to them, "Take courage! I am! Don't be afraid!" And he went up to them, into the boat, and the wind quit.

And they were completely stunned within themselves, for they did not understand about the loaves. Instead, their minds were hardened.

Crossing over to the land, they came to Gennesaret and docked. And when they got out of the boat people immediately recognized Jesus, ran around that whole countryside, and began to carry the sick about on their mats to wherever they heard he was. And wherever he entered, into villages or into cities or into fields, they would put the invalids in the markets and plead with him that they might touch just the edge of his cloak. And as many as touched it were restored.

The Pharisees and some of the legal experts came from Jerusalem and gathered around him. And when they saw that some of his disciples were eating bread with defiled, that is, unwashed, hands—for the Pharisees and all the Jews unless they wash their hands up to the elbow do not eat, thus adhering to the tradition of the elders, and they do not eat anything from the markets unless they purify it, and there are many other things they have received to adhere to, such as purifications for cups and pitchers and kettles—the Pharisees and legal experts asked him, "Why don't your disciples walk according to the tradition of the elders, but instead they eat bread with defiled hands?"

He said to them, "How well Isaiah prophesied about you hypocrites, as it is written,

> 'This people honors me with the lips,
>   but their minds are far away from me.
> In vain they worship me,
>   teaching teachings which are ordinances of men.'

Having left the ordinance of God, you adhere to the tradition of men."

And he said to them, "How well you nullify the ordinance of God in order to establish your tradition! For Moses said, 'Honor your father and your mother' and 'The one who pronounces misfortune upon father or mother must certainly die.' But *you* say that if a man says to his father or his mother 'whatever from me might be a benefit to you is *Corban*'"—that is, a gift consecrated to God—"no longer do you allow him to do anything at all for his father or his mother, thereby invalidating the word of God by your tradition which you have handed on. And you do many such things like this."

And summoning the crowd again, he said to them, "Hear me everyone and understand. There is nothing from outside the man going into him which is able to defile him. Instead, the things going out from the man are the things that defile the man."

When he entered into a house away from the crowd, his disciples were asking him about the riddle. And he said to them, "Do *you* lack understanding like this too? Don't you comprehend that everything that enters into the man from outside isn't able to defile him, because it doesn't enter into his mind but into his stomach and goes out into the toilet?"—thereby pronouncing all foods clean.

He said, "What comes out from the man, *that* defiles the man. For from inside, from the minds of men, come the evil designs: fornications, thefts, murders, adulteries, expressions of greed, malicious deeds, deceit, amorality, an envious eye, blasphemy, arrogance, recklessness. All these wicked things come out from inside and defile the man."

Now from there he rose and went away to the territory of Tyre. And entering into a house, he wanted no one to know about him, but he was not able to escape notice.

Instead, a woman whose little daughter had an unclean spirit immediately heard about him, came, and fell at his feet. Now the woman was Greek, a Syrophoenician by birth, yet she asked him to drive out the demon from her daughter.

And he said to her, "First let the children be satisfied, for it isn't right to take the bread for the children and throw it to the little dogs."

But she answered and said to him, "Lord, even the little dogs down under the table eat the little children's crumbs."

And he said to her, "Because of this word, go off—the demon has gone out from your daughter." And going off to her house, she found the child thrown on the bed and the demon gone out.

Coming back out from the territory of Tyre, he went through Sidon to the Sea of Galilee, up the middle of the territory of the Ten Cities.

And people brought to him a deaf and tongue-tied man and pleaded with Jesus to lay his hand on him. And taking him off from the crowd privately, Jesus thrust his fingers into his ears and with spittle touched the man's tongue. And looking up to heaven, he groaned and said to him, *"Ephphatha!"* which means "Be opened!" And immediately his ears were opened, the binding of his tongue was released, and he began talking clearly.

And Jesus was ordering them to tell no one. But the more he would order them, the more they insisted on proclaiming it. And people were utterly astounded, saying, "How well he does everything. He makes even the deaf hear and the mutes talk."

In those days when again there was a huge crowd and they did not have anything to eat, Jesus summoned the disciples and said to them, "I have compassion for the crowd because already three days they've stayed with me, and they don't have anything to eat. And if I disband them hungry to their houses, they'll become faint on the way. And some of them have come from a distance."

And his disciples answered him, "How will anyone be able to satisfy these people with bread here in a desert?"

And he asked them, "How many loaves have you?"

They said, "Seven."

And he ordered the crowd to recline on the ground. And taking the seven loaves, giving thanks, he broke them, then gave them to his disciples to set out, and they distributed them to the crowd. And they had a few little fish. And blessing them he told the disciples to distribute these also. And people ate and were satisfied.

And the disciples took up seven baskets of scraps. Now there were about four thousand people. And Jesus disbanded them.

Immediately climbing into the boat with his disciples he went to the district of Dalmanutha.

And the Pharisees came out and began to argue with him, seeking from him a sign from heaven, testing him. And groaning deeply in his spirit, he said, "Why does this generation seek a sign? I swear to you, surely a sign won't be given to this generation."

Leaving them, again climbing in, he went off toward the other side. And they forgot to take bread, and except for one loaf they did not have any with them in the boat.

And he was giving them orders, saying, "Beware, look out for the leaven of the Pharisees and the leaven of Herod."

And they began discussing with each other, "We don't have bread."

When Jesus realized this, he said to them, "Why are you discussing that you don't have bread? Don't you comprehend or understand yet? Are your minds hardened? Having eyes, don't you look, and having ears, don't you hear? Don't you remember, when I broke the five loaves for the five thousand, how many baskets full of scraps did you take up?"

They told him, "Twelve."

"When I broke the seven loaves for the four thousand, how many hand-baskets full of scraps did you take up?"

And they said, "Seven."

And he said to them, "Don't you understand yet?"

They came to Bethsaida, and people brought to Jesus a blind man and pleaded with him to touch him. And taking the hand of the blind man, he led him outside the village. And spitting onto his eyes, laying his hands on, he asked him, "Do you see anything?"

And looking up he said, "I see men, but they look like trees walking."

Then again Jesus laid his hands on his eyes, and the man looked intently, then was made new and saw everything clearly. And Jesus sent him to his house, saying, "Don't even enter into the village."

Jesus and his disciples went out to the villages of Caesarea Philippi. And on the way he asked his disciples, saying to them, "Who do men say I am?"

They told him, saying, "John the Baptist, and others say Elijah, but others one of the prophets."

And he asked them, "But who do *you* say I am?"

Peter answered and said to him, "You are the anointed one."

And he rebuked them to tell no one about him, and he began to teach them, "It's necessary for the son of man to suffer greatly, and be rejected by the elders and the high priests and the legal experts, and be put to death, and after three days rise." And he was speaking the word plainly.

And taking him aside, Peter began to rebuke him.

Jesus, turning around and seeing his disciples, rebuked Peter and said, "Get behind me, Satan, because you're not thinking the things of God, but the things of men."

And summoning the crowd with his disciples he said to them, "If anyone wants to follow after me, he is to renounce himself and take up his cross and follow me. For whoever wants to save his life will lose it, but whoever will lose his life for me and the good news will save it. For of what benefit is it for a man to acquire the whole world and forfeit his life? For what would a man give in exchange for his life? For whoever is ashamed of me and my words in this adulterous and sinful generation, also the son of man will be ashamed of him when he comes in the glory of his Father with the holy angels."

And he said to them, "I swear to you that there are some of those standing here who will definitely not taste death before they see the rule of God come in power."

After six days, Jesus took along Peter and James and John and brought them up to a high mountain privately, by themselves. And he was transformed before them, and his clothes became dazzling, intensely white, like no launderer on earth is able to whiten. And Elijah appeared to them with Moses, and they were talking with Jesus.

Peter spoke up and said to Jesus, "Rabbi, it's good *we* are here, and we should make three shelters—one for you and one for Moses and one for Elijah." For he did not know how to respond. For they were so afraid.

And a cloud came overshadowing them, and there was a voice from the cloud, "*This one* is my only son. Hear him." And suddenly, looking around, they no longer saw anyone at all but Jesus alone with them.

While they were coming down from the mountain, Jesus ordered them to recount to no one what they had seen, until after the son of man had risen from the dead.

And they seized on this word, arguing among themselves what "risen from the dead" meant. And they asked him, saying, "Why do the legal experts say that it's necessary for Elijah to come first?"

But he said to them, "If Elijah, coming first, is to put everything right, then how is it written about the son of man that he should suffer greatly and be scorned? On the contrary, I'm telling you that already Elijah has come and they did to him whatever they wanted, just as it's written about him."

Coming to the disciples, they saw a huge crowd around them and legal experts arguing with them. And immediately on seeing him, the whole crowd was alarmed, and running up they began greeting him.

And he asked them, "What are you arguing about with them?"

And someone from the crowd answered him, "Teacher, I brought my son to you, because he has a mute spirit. And wherever it takes hold of him, it hurls him down, and he foams at the mouth and grinds his teeth, then withers up. And I told your disciples to drive it out, and they weren't strong enough."

He answered them and said, "O faithless generation, how long am I to be with you? How long am I to put up with you? Bring him to me." And they brought the child to him.

And upon seeing Jesus, the spirit immediately convulsed the child, and he fell to the ground and was writhing about, foaming at the mouth.

And Jesus asked his father, "How long has it been like this with him?"

He said, "From childhood. And often it has thrown him even into fire and into water in order to destroy him. But if you're able to do anything, have compassion for us and help us."

Jesus said to him, "'If you're able'? Everything is possible to one who has faith."

Immediately the father of the child screamed and said, "I have faith. Help my lack of faith."

Now when Jesus saw that a crowd was running together, he rebuked the unclean spirit, saying to it, "Mute and deaf spirit, *I* order you: Come out from him and never enter into him again!" And screaming and convulsing him violently, it came out.

And the child became so like a dead person that most said, "He died." But Jesus, grasping his hand, raised him up, and he rose.

And when Jesus entered into a house, his disciples privately asked him, "Why weren't *we* able to drive it out?"

And he said to them, "This kind it isn't possible for anyone to drive out, except by prayer."

Going out from there, they were passing through Galilee, and he did not want anyone to know, for he was teaching his disciples and telling them, "The son of man is to be handed over to the hands of men, and they will put him to death, and three days after being put to death he will rise." But they did not comprehend the saying and were afraid to ask him.

They came to Capernaum. And when he was in the house, he asked them, "What were you discussing on the way?"

But they kept quiet, for they had discussed with each other on the way who was greatest.

And sitting down he called the twelve and said to them, "If anyone wants to be most important, he will be least of all and everyone's servant."

And taking a little child he stood it in their midst, and putting his arms around it he said to them, "Whoever receives one such little child in my name is receiving me, and whoever receives me is receiving not me but the One who sent me."

John said to him, "Teacher, we saw someone driving out demons in your name, and we were stopping him, because he wasn't following us."

But Jesus said, "Don't stop him. For there is no one who will do a work of power by my name and be able soon after to pronounce misfortune on me. For whoever isn't against us is for us. For whoever offers you a cup of water based on a name, because you belong to the anointed one, I swear to you that he will definitely not lose his reward. And whoever causes one of these little ones who have faith to stumble, it would be better for him instead if a large millstone had been tied around his neck and he had been thrown into the sea.

"And if your hand causes you to stumble, cut it off! It's better for you to enter into life maimed, than with two hands to go off to Gehenna, to the inextinguishable fire. And if your foot causes you to stumble, cut it off! It's better for you to enter into life lame, than with two feet to be thrown into Gehenna. And if your eye causes you to stumble, pull it out! It's better for you with one eye to enter into the rule of God than with two eyes to be thrown into Gehenna, where their maggots don't die and the fire isn't extinguished.

"For everyone will be salted with fire. Salt is good. But if salt become saltless, how will you make it season? Have salt among yourselves and be at peace with each other."

From there he arose and went to the region of Judea and across the Jordan. Again crowds gathered around him, and as it had been his custom, again he was teaching them.

Pharisees approached and asked him if it were legal for a husband to divorce his wife, testing him.

Answering, he said to them, "What did Moses order you?"

They said, "Moses permitted him to write a certificate of divorce and to divorce her."

Jesus said to them, "Because of your callous minds he wrote you this ordinance. But from the beginning of creation, He made them male and female. For this reason a man will leave his father and mother behind, and the two will be as one flesh, so that no longer are they two, but one flesh. So, what God yoked together, a man is not to separate."

And in the house again, the disciples asked him about this. And he said to them, "Whoever divorces his wife and marries another commits adultery against her. And if that woman divorcing her husband marries another, she commits adultery."

People were bringing to him little children so he might touch them. But the disciples rebuked them.

Now when Jesus saw it, he got angry and said to them, "Let the little children come to me. Don't stop them. For the rule of God belongs to such as these. I swear to you that whoever does not receive the rule of God like a little child will definitely not enter into it." And putting his arms around them, he laid his hands on them, and was blessing them profusely.

As he was setting out on the way, someone ran up and falling on his knees before him asked him, "Good teacher, what am I to do in order to inherit eternal life?"

22

Jesus said to him, "Why do you say I'm good? No one is good except the one God. You know the ordinances: don't murder, don't commit adultery, don't steal, don't testify falsely, don't defraud, honor your father and mother."

He said to Jesus, "Teacher, all these I've kept from my youth."

Jesus, looking at him intently, loved him, then said to him, "One thing you lack. Go sell whatever you have and give to the poor, and you'll have a fortune in heaven, and come follow me."

But becoming dejected at this word he went away sad, for he had a lot of property.

And looking around Jesus said to his disciples, "How hard it will be for those who have possessions to enter into the rule of God!" Now the disciples were astonished at his words.

Jesus again spoke up and said to them, "Children, how hard it is to enter into the rule of God! It's easier for a camel to go through an eye of a needle, than for a wealthy man to enter into the rule of God."

But they were completely astounded, saying among themselves, "So who is able to be saved?"

Looking at them intently, Jesus said, "To men it's impossible, but not to God, for everything is possible to God."

Peter began to say to him, "Look, *we* left everything and have followed you."

Jesus said, "I swear to you that there is no one who has left a house or brothers or sisters or a mother or a father or children or fields for me and for the good news who does not receive a hundred times as many now, in this time, houses and brothers and sisters and mothers and fathers and children and fields—with persecutions—and in the coming age, eternal life. But many who are most important will be least and the least, most important."

Now they were on the way going up to Jerusalem, and Jesus was going ahead of them, and they were astonished, and those following were afraid.

And again taking the twelve aside he began to tell them the things which were about to happen to him, "Look, we're going up to Jerusalem, and the son of man will be handed over to the high priests and the legal experts, and they will condemn him to death and hand him over to the gentiles, and they will mock him and spit on him and flog him, then put him to death, and after three days, he will rise."

And James and John the sons of Zebedee approached him, saying to him, "Teacher, we want you to do for us whatever we ask of you."

He said to them, "What do you want me to do for you?"

They said to him, "Give us a place to sit, one on your right and one on your left, in your glory."

Jesus said to them, "You don't know what you're asking for. Are you able to drink the cup that I am to drink or be baptized with the baptism by which I am to be baptized?"

They said to him, "We're able."

Jesus said to them, "The cup that I am to drink, you will drink, and with the baptism by which I am to be baptized, you will be baptized, but to sit on my right or on the left is not mine to give, but is for those for whom it has been prepared."

And when the ten heard, they began to get angry at James and John.

And summoning them, Jesus said to them, "You know that those who seem to rule the gentile nations lord over them, and their great ones exert authority over them, but it's not to be like this among you. Instead, whoever wants to be great among you will be your servant, and whoever wants to be most important among you will be everyone's slave. For even the son of man came not to be served, but to serve and to give his life a ransom for many."

They came to Jericho. And as he was going out from Jericho with his disciples and a sizable crowd, the son of Timaeus—Bartimaeus, a blind man—was sitting beside the way, begging.

And hearing that it was Jesus the Nazarene, he began to scream, and say, "Son of David! Jesus! Show me mercy!"

And many were rebuking him to be quiet, but he kept screaming that much more, "Son of David! Show me mercy!"

And stopping, Jesus said, "Call him."

And they called the blind man, saying to him, "Take courage. Rise. He's calling you." And throwing off his cloak, he jumped up and went to Jesus.

And responding to him, Jesus said, "What do you want me to do for you?"

The blind man said to him, "Rabboni, that I might see again."

And Jesus said to him, "Go off, your faith has restored you."

And immediately he saw again and began following Jesus on the way.

When they came near to Jerusalem, to Bethphage and Bethania, at the Mountain of the Olives, he sent two of his disciples and said to them, "Go into the village opposite you, and immediately as you're entering into it you'll find a donkey colt tied up on which no one has ever yet sat. Untie it and bring it. And if anyone says to you, 'Why are you doing this?' say, 'The lord has a need for it and will immediately send it back here.'"

And they went off and found a colt tied up at a door outside on the street, and they untied it. And some of those standing there said to them, "What are you doing untying the colt?" The disciples told them just as Jesus had said, and they let them take it.

And they brought the colt to Jesus, then threw their cloaks over it, and he sat on it. And many spread their cloaks onto the way, while others spread leafy branches cut from the fields. And those going ahead and those following were screaming,

"Hosanna!

Blessed is the one coming in the Lord's name!

Blessed is the coming rule of our father David!

Hosanna in the highest places!"

And he entered into Jerusalem, into the temple. And after looking around at everything, the hour being already late, he went out to Bethania with the twelve.

On the following day, when they came out from Bethania, he was hungry. And seeing from a distance a fig tree with leaves, he went to see if perhaps he might find some fruit on it. And coming to it, he found nothing except leaves (for it was not the right time for figs).

And reacting he said to it, "May no one any longer ever eat fruit from you again." And his disciples heard.

They came to Jerusalem. And entering into the temple he began to drive out those selling and those buying in the temple, and he upended the tables of those changing money and the chairs of those selling doves, and he would not let anyone take a vessel across the temple.

And he began teaching, and said to them, "Isn't it written, 'My house shall be called a house of prayer for all the gentile nations'? But *you* have made it a lair for bandits."

And the high priests and the legal experts heard and began seeking how they might destroy him. For they were afraid of him. For the whole crowd was astounded at his teaching. And when evening came, they went outside the city.

Passing by early in the morning, they saw the fig tree withered to the roots. And remembering, Peter said to him, "Rabbi, look, the fig tree which you cursed has withered!"

And answering, Jesus said to them, "Have faith in God. I swear to you that whoever says to this mountain 'Be taken up and thrown into the sea,' and doesn't doubt in his mind but has faith that what he says will happen, it will be so for him. Therefore, I'm telling you, regarding everything you pray for and ask for, have faith that you have gotten it, and it will be so for you. And when you stand praying, pardon whatever you have against anyone, so that also your Father who is in heaven may pardon you your offenses."

They came back into Jerusalem. And while he was walking in the temple, the high priests and the legal experts and the elders came to him, and they said to him, "By what authority are you doing these things? Or who gave you this authority to do these things?"

Jesus said to them, "I'll ask you one question. Answer me, and I'll tell you by what authority I do these things. Was the baptism of John from heaven or from men? Answer me."

And they began discussing among themselves, saying, "If we say 'From heaven,' he'll say, 'Then why didn't you put faith in him?' But, if we say, 'From men' . . ."—they were afraid of the crowd, for everyone held that John really was a prophet.

And answering Jesus, they said, "We don't know."

And Jesus said to them, "Then neither am *I* telling you by what authority I do these things."

And he began to tell them in riddles: "A man planted a vineyard and put a wall around it and dug out a wine pit and built a watch tower, then leased it out to farmers and went away. And he sent to the farmers at the right time a slave in order to get from the farmers some of the fruits of the vineyard. And taking him, they flogged him and sent him away empty-handed. And again he sent to them another slave, and that one they struck in the head and dishonored. And he sent another, and that one they put to death. And many others, some they flogged and some they put to death.

"Still he had one more, an only son. He sent him last to them, saying, 'They will have regard for my son.' But those farmers said to themselves, 'This one is the heir. Come on, let's put him to death, and the inheritance will be ours.' And taking him they put him to death and threw him outside the vineyard.

"So what will the lord of the vineyard do? He'll come and destroy the farmers and give the vineyard to others. Haven't you read this writing:
'That stone which the builders rejected
    became the cornerstone.
This came from the Lord
    and it is amazing in our eyes'?"

And they began seeking to seize him, yet they feared the crowd, for they knew that Jesus told the riddle against them. And leaving him, they went off.

And they sent to him some of the Pharisees and the Herodians to catch him in his words. And coming, they said to him, "Teacher, we know that you are truthful and don't defer to anyone, for you don't look to the reaction of men, but truthfully teach the way of God. Is it legal to give a tribute payment to Caesar or not? Should we give or not give?"

But seeing their hypocrisy he said to them, "Why are you testing me? Bring me a denarius so I might see." They brought one.

And he said to them, "Whose image is this and whose inscription?"

They told him, "Caesar's."

Jesus said to them, "The things of Caesar give back to Caesar and the things of God to God." And they were utterly amazed at him.

Sadducees, who say there is no resurrection, came to him and asked him, saying, "Teacher, Moses wrote for us 'if someone's brother dies and leaves a wife behind but doesn't leave a child, then his brother is to take the wife and raise up a descendant for his brother.' There were seven brothers. And the first took a wife and when he died didn't leave a descendant. And the second took her, and he died without leaving behind a descendant. And the third did likewise. And none of the seven left a descendant. Last of all, also the wife died. In the resurrection, when they rise, whose wife will she be? For the seven had her as a wife."

Jesus said to them, "Aren't you misled because of this—you know neither the writings nor the power of God? For when people rise from the dead, they neither marry nor are given for marriage, but are like angels in heaven. Now as for the dead, that they rise, haven't you read in the book from Moses, in the passage about the bush, how God told him, saying, 'I am the

God of Abraham and the God of Isaac and the God of Jacob'? He isn't God of dead people but of living people. You're greatly misled."

One of the legal experts approached, heard them arguing, saw how well Jesus was answering them, and asked him, "Which is the most important ordinance of all?"

Jesus answered, "The most important is, 'Hear, Israel, the Lord our God is one Lord, and you are to love the Lord your God with your whole mind and with your whole life and with your whole intelligence and with your whole strength.' The second is this, 'You are to love your neighbor as yourself.' There is not another ordinance greater than these."

And the legal expert said to him, "How well you say truthfully, teacher, that He is one and there is not another except Him, and to love Him with the whole mind and with the whole understanding and with the whole strength, and to love the neighbor as oneself is much more than all the whole burnt offerings and sacrifices."

And seeing that he had answered wisely, Jesus said to him, "You're not far from the rule of God." And no one any longer had courage to ask him anything.

And responding, Jesus said while teaching in the temple, "How do the legal experts say that the anointed one is a son of David? David himself said by the holy spirit,

'The Lord said to my lord,
'Sit on my right
until I put your enemies down under your feet.'

David himself calls him 'lord,' so how is he his son?" And the huge crowd was glad to hear him.

In his teaching, he said, "Look out for some of the legal experts, the ones who want to walk about in flowing robes and want formal greetings in the markets and most important seats in the synagogues and most important places at the banquets. The ones who eat up the houses of the widows and for appearance offer long prayers, *they* will get a more severe condemnation."

Sitting opposite the sacred treasury, he began observing how the crowd put money into the treasury box. And many wealthy people were putting in large amounts. And one poor widow came and put in two little coppers, which make a quadrans.

And summoning his disciples, he said to them, "I swear to you that this poor widow put in more than everyone else who put into the treasury. For everyone else put in from their surplus, but this woman from her need put in everything she had, her whole living."

And as he was coming out from the temple, one of his disciples said to him, "Teacher, look! What stones and what buildings!"

And Jesus said to him, "You see these great buildings? Definitely not a stone will be left upon a stone here which will not definitely be pulled down."

While he was sitting on the Mountain of the Olives, facing the temple, Peter and James and John and Andrew asked him privately, "Tell us, when will these things be? And what will the sign be when these things are all about to be brought to an end?"

Jesus began to tell them, "Look out that no one mislead you. Many will come in my name, saying, 'I am' and mislead many.

"Now when you hear battles and reports of battles, don't be alarmed. It's necessary for these to happen, but it's not yet the end. For nation will rise against nation and realm against realm. There will be earthquakes in different places. There will be famines. These are a beginning of birth pains.

"Now you look out for yourselves. They will hand you over to sanhedrins and you'll be beaten in synagogues and you'll stand before governors and kings for me, as testimony to them. And it's necessary first for the good news to be proclaimed among all the gentile nations. And when they lead you away, handing you over, don't be anxious ahead about what you are to say. Instead, say whatever is given to you in that hour, for *you* won't be the ones speaking, but the holy spirit. And brother will hand over brother to death, and a father his child, and children will rise in rebellion against parents and have them put to death. And you will be hated by everyone because of my name. But whoever endures to the end will be saved.

"Now when you see the 'horror of desolation' standing where it's necessary that it not stand"—let the reader comprehend—"at that time those in Judea are to flee to the mountains. Whoever is on the roof is to come down without entering to take something from his house, and whoever is in the field is not to turn back to take his cloak. How awful for those who are pregnant and those nursing a child in those days! Pray that it not happen in winter. For those days will be an oppression the like of which hasn't happened from the beginning of creation which God created until now and definitely won't happen again. And if the Lord had not cut short the days, no flesh would be saved at all. But because of the chosen ones whom he chose, he cut short the days.

"And at that time if anyone says to you, 'Look, here is the anointed one! Look, there he is!' don't put faith in it. For false anointed ones and false prophets will rise up and give signs and portents to lead astray, if possible, the chosen ones. But you look out! I've told you everything ahead.

"However, in those days, after that oppression,
'the sun will be darkened,
and the moon won't give its light
and the stars will be falling from the heaven,
and the powers in the heavens will be shaken.'
And at that time people will behold the son of man coming in clouds with tremendous power and glory. And at that time he will send the angels and gather together the chosen ones from the four winds, from the extremity of earth to the extremity of heaven.

"Now from the fig tree, learn the riddle. When already its shoots have become tender and it is putting out the leaves, you know that the summer is near. So also you, when you see these things happening, you are to know that he is near, at the doors. I swear to you that this generation will definitely not pass away before all these things happen. The heaven and the earth will pass away, but my words will definitely not pass away.

"Now about that day or the hour, no one knows—neither the angels in heaven nor the son—except the Father. Look out, stay awake, for you don't know when the right time will be. It's like a man away: leaving his house and giving his slaves the authority, to each his work, he ordered also the doorkeeper to keep watch. So keep watch, for you don't know when the lord of the house is coming, whether in the evening or in the middle of the night or at the rooster crow or early in the morning. Otherwise he might come unexpectedly and find you sleeping.

"Now what I say to you, I'm saying to everyone, keep watch!"

Now the Passover festival and the festival of Unleavened Bread were two days away. And the high priests and the legal experts were seeking how to seize him by deceit and put him to death. For they were saying, "Not among the festival crowd, otherwise there will be a disturbance of the populace."

Jesus was in Bethania, in the house of Simon the leper. While he was reclining to eat, a woman came who had an alabaster flask of very expensive, pure nard ointment. Breaking open the alabaster flask she began pouring ointment on his head.

Now some were angry among themselves, "Why has this ointment been wasted? For this ointment could have been sold for over three hundred denarii and the money given to the poor." And they were harsh with her.

Jesus said, "Let her be. Why are you giving her trouble? It's a good work she did for me. For the poor you always have with you and whenever you want you're able to do good for them, but me you won't always have. What she was able to do, she did. She anointed my body ahead for the burial. I swear to you, wherever the good news is proclaimed in the whole world, what she did will also be told as a remembrance of her."

And Judas Iscariot, the one of the twelve, went off to the high priests to hand Jesus over to them. Now when they heard, they rejoiced and promised to give him silver. And he began seeking how at some opportunity he might hand him over.

On the first day of the festival of Unleavened Bread, when it was customary to slaughter the Passover lamb, his disciples said to him, "Where do you want us to go off and prepare for you to eat the Passover meal?"

And he sent two of his disciples and said to them, "Go to the city, and a man carrying a jar of water will meet you. Follow him and where he enters tell the master of the house, 'The teacher says, "Where is my guestroom where I am to eat the Passover meal with my disciples?"' And he will show you a large upstairs room furnished and ready, and there prepare for us."

And the disciples went out and came to the city and found things just as he told them and prepared the Passover meal.

29

When it was evening, he came with the twelve. And while they were reclining and eating, Jesus said, "I swear to you that one of you will hand me over, one eating with me."

They began to be sad and to say to him one after another, "Surely not I?"

He said to them, "One of the twelve, the one dipping bread with me in the bowl. The son of man goes just as it is written about him, but how awful for that man by whom the son of man is handed over. Better for that man if he had not been born."

While they were eating, he took bread, blessed it, broke it, then gave it to them and said, "Take it. This is my body."

And taking a cup, offering thanks, he gave it to them, and everyone drank from it. And he said to them, "This is my blood of the covenant which is about to be poured out for many. I swear to you that I definitely won't any longer drink from the produce of the vine until that day when I drink it new in the rule of God."

And after singing a psalm, they went out to the Mountain of the Olives. And Jesus said to them, "You will all stumble, because it is written,

'I will strike the shepherd
and the sheep will be scattered.'

However, after I'm raised, I'll go ahead of you to Galilee."

Peter said to him, "Even if everyone else stumbles, at least *I* won't.

And Jesus said to him, "I swear to you that today, this night, before the rooster crows twice, *you* will renounce me three times."

But he kept saying wildly, "Even if it's necessary for me to die with you, I'll definitely not renounce you." And everyone was saying the same.

They came to a place which had the name Gethsemane, and he said to his disciples, "Sit here while I pray."

And he took along Peter and James and John with him, and he began to be alarmed and anguished, and he said to them, "My life is profoundly sad to death. Stay here and keep watch."

And going ahead a little, he fell to the ground and began praying that, if it were possible, the hour might pass away from him, and he said, "*Abba,* Father, everything is possible for you. Take this cup away from me, yet not what *I* want, but what *you* want."

And he came and found them sleeping, and he said to Peter, "Simon, are you sleeping? Weren't you strong enough to keep watch one hour? Keep watch, and pray that you don't come to a testing. The spirit is eager, but the flesh weak."

And again going off, he prayed, saying the same words. And again he came and found them sleeping, for their eyes were very heavy, and they did not know what to answer him.

And he came the third time and said to them, "Are you going to sleep through and keep resting? It's over! The hour came! Look, the son of man is about to be handed over to the hands of the sinners! Rise! Let's go! Look, the one handing me over has come near!"

And immediately while he was still talking Judas, one of the twelve, arrived and with him a crowd with swords and clubs from the high priests and the legal experts and the elders.

Now the one handing him over had given them a signal, saying, "He is the one I'll kiss. Seize him and lead him away under security."

And coming, immediately approaching him, he said, "Rabbi" and kissed him dramatically. And they put hands on him and seized him. But one of those standing by drew his sword, struck the slave of the high priest, and cut off a little piece of his ear.

And reacting, Jesus said to them, "As against a bandit did you come out with swords and clubs to capture me? Day after day I was among you in the temple teaching, and you didn't seize me. However, so the writings might be fulfilled." And leaving him, everyone fled.

And a certain young man was following him wearing a linen cloth around his naked body, and they seized him. But leaving the linen cloth behind, he fled naked.

They led Jesus away to the High Priest, and all the high priests and the elders and the legal experts assembled. And Peter followed him from a distance on inside to the courtyard of the High Priest, and he was sitting together with the guards and warming himself in the firelight.

Now the high priests and the whole sanhedrin were seeking testimony against Jesus to have him put to death, but they were not finding any. For many were testifying falsely against him, and their testimony would not agree.

And some rose and testified falsely against him, saying, "We ourselves heard him saying, '*I* will pull down this sanctuary made with hands and in three days build another not made with hands.'" But not even on this point did their testimony agree.

And rising to the center, the High Priest asked Jesus, saying, "Aren't you answering anything at all? What are these men testifying against you?" But he kept quiet and did not answer anything at all.

Again the High Priest asked him and said to him, "Are *you* the anointed one, the son of the Blessed One?"

Jesus said, "I am,
and you will behold the son of man
sitting on the right of the Powerful One
and coming with the clouds of heaven."

The High Priest, tearing his vestments, said, "What further need have we for witnesses? You heard the blasphemy! How does it appear to you?" And they all condemned him to be deserving of death. And some began to spit on him and cover his face, then hit him and say to him, "Prophesy!" And the guards took to beating him.

Peter was down in the courtyard, when one of the maids of the High Priest came. And seeing Peter warming himself, she looked intently at him and said, "*You* too were with the Nazarene Jesus."

But he denied it, saying, "I don't know or understand what you're talking about." And he went outside to the forecourt. And a rooster crowed. And the maid saw him, and began again to say to those standing by, "This is one of them." But again he denied it.

And after a little while again those standing by began saying to Peter, "Truthfully you're one of them, for you too are a Galilean." But he began to put himself under a curse and to swear an oath, "I don't know this man you're talking about." And immediately for the second time a rooster crowed. And Peter remembered the saying, how Jesus had said to him, "Before a rooster crows twice, you'll renounce me three times." And lurching off, he began sobbing.

Immediately, early in the morning, the high priests held a council with the elders and legal experts and the whole Sanhedrin, bound Jesus, took him away, and handed him over to Pilate.

And Pilate asked him, "Are *you* the king of the Jews?"

Answering him, he said, "*You* are saying so."

And the high priests were bringing many charges against him. Pilate again asked him, saying, "Aren't you answering anything at all? Look how many charges they're bringing against you!"

But Jesus no longer answered anything at all, with the result that Pilate was amazed.

Now at festivals, he would release for them one prisoner whom they requested. Now the one called Barabbas was bound in prison with the insurrectionists who had committed murder in the insurrection. And coming up, the crowd began to ask Pilate to do just as he customarily did for them.

Pilate answered them, saying, "Do you want me to release for you the king of the Jews?" For he knew that on account of envy the high priests had handed him over.

But the high priests stirred up the crowd to have him instead release Barabbas to them.

Pilate again spoke up and said to them, "Then what should I do with the king of the Jews?"

They screamed back, "Crucify him!"

Pilate said to them, "Why, what harm did he do?"

But they screamed all the louder, "Crucify him!"

Now Pilate, wishing to do the satisfactory thing for the crowd, released to them Barabbas, and whipping Jesus, handed him over to be crucified.

Now the soldiers led him away inside the courtyard (which is a praetorium), and they called together the whole cohort. And they put a purple cloak on him and they set on him a crown woven from thorns. And they began to greet him, "Hail, king of the Jews!" And they were beating his head with a reed pole and spitting on him, and getting on their knees, they were giving him obeisance. And when they had mocked him, they took the purple cloak off him and put his own clothes on him, then led him out to crucify him.

And they drafted a passerby, a certain Simon Cyrenean, coming from the countryside (the father of Alexander and Rufus), to take up his cross. And they brought Jesus to the place Golgotha, which means "Place of the Skull." And they tried giving him wine drugged with myrrh, but he did not take it.
And they crucified him,
     and they divided up his clothes,
       casting lots for them, who might take what.
Now it was nine in the morning when they crucified him. And the inscription of the charge against him was inscribed THE KING OF THE JEWS. With him they crucified two bandits, one on the right and one on his left.

And those going by were blaspheming him, wagging their heads and saying, "Ha! The one who's about to pull down the sanctuary and build one in three days! Save yourself by getting down off the cross!"

Likewise also the high priests mocking him to each other with the legal experts were saying, "Others he restored; himself he isn't able to save. Let the anointed one, the king of Israel, get down now off the cross, so we might see and have faith." Even those crucified along with him were ridiculing him.

When it was noon, a darkness came over the whole land until three. And at three Jesus shouted in a loud cry, *"Eloi! Eloi! Lama sabachthani?"* which means "My God! My God! Why did you abandon me?"

And some of those standing by heard it and said, "Look, he's calling Elijah!" Someone ran, filled a sponge with cheap wine, put it on a reed pole, and offered him a drink, saying "Let him be! Let's see if Elijah comes to get him down."

But Jesus, letting out a loud cry, died.

And the curtain of the sanctuary was ripped in two from top to bottom.

Now when the centurion who was standing in front of him saw that he died like this, he said, "Truthfully this man was a son of God."

Now there were also women observing from a distance, among them Mary the Magdalene and Mary the mother of James the lesser and of Joses and Salome, who were following him and serving him when he was in Galilee, and many other women who came up with him to Jerusalem.

It was already evening and since it was preparation day (that is, a day before the Sabbath), Joseph from Arimathea, a prominent council member who also was himself expecting the rule of God, came and taking courage went in to Pilate and asked for the body of Jesus. Now Pilate was amazed that he had already died, and summoning the centurion he asked him whether he had been dead long. And finding out from the centurion, he granted the corpse to Joseph.

And buying a linen cloth, taking him down, Joseph wrapped him in the linen cloth and put him in a grave which had been hewn out of rock, then rolled a stone up against the door of the grave. Now Mary the Magdalene and Mary the mother of Joses were observing where he was put.

When the Sabbath passed, Mary the Magdalene and Mary the mother of

James and Salome bought aromatic oils so they might go anoint him. And very early in the morning, on the first day after the Sabbath, they went toward the grave as the sun came up.

And they were saying to themselves, "Who will roll away for us the stone from the door of the grave?" And looking up they observed that the stone had been rolled away. For it was very large.

And entering into the grave they saw a young man sitting to the right wearing a white robe, and they were alarmed.

He said to them, "Don't be alarmed. You're seeking Jesus the Nazarene who was crucified. He was raised! He's not here! Look, the place where they put him! But go tell his disciples, even Peter, 'He's going ahead of you to Galilee. There you will behold him, just as he told you.'"

But coming out they fled from the grave, for they were trembling and stunned. And they said nothing at all to anyone, for they were afraid.

2

The Rhetoric

What is it about the way this story is told that evokes in the reader suspense or amazement or fear or surprise? How does the story lead the reader to align with Jesus and to distrust the authorities? How does the narrator establish authority with the reader? What literary devices does the narrator use to hold the reader's attention from one episode to another? These are questions about *rhetoric*, about "how" the story is told to create certain effects on the reader. Obviously in a brief study of the whole story we can only illustrate the characteristics of rhetorical devices such as the narrator, the style, and narrative patterns. Yet an understanding of these rhetorical techniques is important to the interpretation of every episode. Also, our analysis of the rhetoric informs the subsequent discussion of the story at many significant points.

THE NARRATOR

The "narrator" is a literary term for the storyteller of a narrative. The narrator is not the author but a rhetorical device the author uses to get the story told and to get it told in a certain way.[1]

There are several kinds of narrators. The narrator may be a character in the story, the protagonist, or perhaps a peripheral character. Such "I-we" or first-person narrators are common. Mark Twain, for example, has Huck narrate *Huckleberry Finn* and J. D. Salinger has Holden Caulfield narrate *Catcher in the Rye*. There are limitations to the way character-narrators tell a story. Huck, for example, can tell only what he himself has seen or heard, what he—but no other character—is thinking, and what his own limited values or experiences will enable him to understand. The reader is aware of Huck's limitations and evaluates how much this imaginative youth understands and how much he distorts what he recounts.

Other kinds of narrators are not characters. They are unnamed narrators outside the story being told, but still evident in the narrative as the storyteller. These are omniscient narrators. The reader is not usually aware of an omniscient narrator any more than one is aware of a movie camera while watching a film. A narrator with "objective omniscience" can tell everything which can be seen and heard, without showing what is in the minds of the characters. Ernest Hemingway, for example, uses an objective narrator to tell many of his stories. A narrator with "limited omniscience," in addition to objective-style description, also tells thoughts and feelings, but only those in the mind of the protagonist. A narrator displaying "unlimited omniscience" may tell anything about the story world, including what is in the mind of any character at any time and place. Most stories, including such works as Homer's *Odyssey,* Tolstoy's *War and Peace,* and *The Gospel of Mark* are told by an unlimited omniscient narrator.

The salient features of Mark's narrator are these: the narrator does not figure in the events of the story; speaks in the third person; is not bound by time or space in the telling of the story; is an implied invisible presence in every scene, capable of being anywhere to "recount" the action; displays full omniscience by narrating the thoughts, feelings, or sensory experiences of many characters; often turns from the story to give direct "asides" to the reader, explaining a custom or translating a word or commenting on the story; and narrates the story from one overarching ideological point of view. Understanding these characteristics enables the reader to see how the omniscient narrator guides the reader through the world of the story.[2]

Mark's narrator is omniscient. The rhetorical characteristics of an unlimited omniscient narrator are consistent throughout Mark's narrative. A simple exercise will reveal the role of the omniscient narrator in Mark's story in contrast to the role of a first-person narrator. In an episode in which Jesus appears one could read the story from his point of view by substituting "I" or "we" where "Jesus" or "he" or "they" appear. This can also be done for an opponent or a disciple. This shift in perspective significantly changes one's experience of the story. It shows how the omniscient narrator speaks in the third person from outside the story and does not figure in the story as a character-narrator would. And it reveals the unlimited knowledge of the omniscient narrator because no character has enough knowledge of other characters or events to be able to tell the whole story as the omniscient narrator has told it.

The narrator is not bound by time or space. Mark's narrator tells the story in the past tense. So, in the context of the story world, the narrator speaks from a temporal point of view sometime after the episode of the empty tomb and presumably before the rule of God is to be fully established within a generation. From this point in the continuum of the story world, the narrator knows the whole story, including the imaginative past time and the imaginative future time of the story world, and is, therefore, not bound by time in the telling of that story. The narrator can at any point in the story relate to the reader something that had happened earlier (such as John's death) or tell ahead of time what will happen later (such as Judas's handing Jesus over).

Nor is Mark's narrator limited by space. The narrator knows what happens in every place, unlike a character-narrator who would have to be present or hear about an event indirectly in order to be able to recount it realistically. Thus, the omniscient narrator can depict not only public events but also what happens privately in houses or on a boat or in the desert—not only when Jesus is with someone, but also when he is alone. The narrator depicts *mostly* scenes in which Jesus is present, but can also shift to other settings instantaneously to depict the high priests plotting against Jesus, or Peter denying Jesus.

The narrator narrates the story with a temporal and spatial immediacy as of one invisibly present to recount what is occurring in each successive episode of the story. Because the reader experiences the story as the narrator tells it, the reader also has the sense of being invisibly present to witness these events of the story world.

The narrator gives "inside views" of the characters' minds. For example, the narrator shows the reader that the opponents think Jesus is a blasphemer, that Herod considers John to be a just man, and that Pilate knows the high priests are envious.[3] The narrator also describes the innermost feelings of the characters: their compassion, anger, astonishment, fear, sadness, amazement, or love; and tells when they are dazed, stunned, puzzled, pleased, terrified, or dejected. The narrator explains when characters do not understand or do not know what to say. The narrator even reveals that the minds of the disciples are hardened when not even the disciples themselves (or Jesus) are aware of it.

This unlimited knowledge of the omniscient narrator, unbound by time or space and able to know the minds of the characters, gives the narrator tremendous authority with the reader, who comes to trust the narrator as a reliable guide in the world of the story. Furthermore, seeing the story from the point of view of the narrator gives the reader an advantage over the characters in the story, who usually cannot know what other characters are thinking and often do not know what other characters are doing.

The narrator speaks to the reader through "asides." Through most of the story, the narrator is occupied with narrating the dialogue or thoughts or actions of the characters. The reader is caught up in the story itself, unaware of the narrator. Occasionally, however, the narrator addresses the reader directly, making comments or explanations which do not figure as part of the events themselves and which often include information not even available to characters in the story.[4] The phrasing of these asides usually confirms that it is the narrator speaking and not one of the characters. Literary asides resemble the feature of some films in which a voice from an unidentified source speaks occasionally to comment on the story being shown.

In Mark's story, these asides are like brief interruptions in the description of events, sometimes indicated by an abrupt break in the syntax of the sentence, followed by the narrator's comment. For example, after Jesus explains the riddle about what defiles, the narrator gives an aside which offers further commentary, that Jesus was "pronouncing all foods clean." When Jesus is prophesying to his disciples about the "horror of desolation," the narrator breaks in abruptly with the comment, "let the reader comprehend," thus alerting the reader to understand the special significance of this phrase. Other asides simply aid the reader's understanding of various aspects of the story world. The narrator explains that "defiled hands" are unwashed hands, that Sadducees do not believe in a resurrection, that a certain courtyard is a praetorium, and so on. Seven times, in relative clauses, the narrator translates the meaning of Aramaic words in the narrative. Also, the narrator often comments on a surprising action or statement that a reader might misunderstand, with explanations that are usually introduced by the conjunction "for," as when the narrator explains that a little girl raised from the dead was able to walk, "for she was twelve years old," and that the fig tree did not have any fruit on it, "for it was not the right time for figs."[5]

By itself an intrusion or "aside" may or may not be significant, but the overall impact of these asides is certainly significant. The inclusion of details such as foreign words and customs makes the story more realistic and authentic. Also, when the narrator turns aside from recounting the story in order to comment to the reader directly, the reader becomes aware of the presence of a narrator and aware that the narrator is guiding the reader through the story. The reader comes to rely on the narrator to provide reliable commentary on the story. In this way the narrator's increasing influence over the reader's responses encourages the reader to accept other judgments the narrator makes about events and characters in the course of narration.

The narrator speaks from an ideological point of view. When the narrator is omniscient and invisible, readers tend to be unaware of the narrator's biases, values, and conceptual view of the world. The reader tends to trust the narrator as a disinterested observer of the events of the story. But the omniscient narrator is not a disinterested observer. Rather, the narrator functions as would the director of a movie, as someone who is responsible for the presentation of the whole story. Viewers observe the scenes and characters from the director's perspective, although they never see the director. Similarly, the narrator of a story in literature is responsible not just for the asides but for the presentation of the whole story. The narrator narrates the story with certain loaded words, in a certain order, and with various rhetorical techniques. So the narrator is always there at the reader's elbow shaping responses to the story— even, and perhaps especially, when the reader is least aware of it.

To be aware of the ideological point of view of the narrator in Mark's story, imagine that story being told by an omniscient narrator whose sympathies lie with the Pharisees and the high priests. The reader's experience of the story would be entirely different. Although the same basic story line and plotted events would be described, the words chosen to describe them would vary so as to give a different perspective to the drama. Now if we think again about Mark's story, we can see how much of the point of view is not neutral. For example, the narrator does not give disinterested portrayals so that the readers can decide for themselves about the characters; the narrator clearly favors some characters over others. Also, the narrator guides the reader's attitude toward the different characters by telling in a variety of ways who the "good" characters are and who the "bad" ones are in the story world.

We can discern the narrator's views toward a character from the way in which the narrator introduces that character into the narrative and provides views into the mind of that character. An example of this occurs when the narrator introduces Jesus in the first line as "the anointed one, the son of God," then confirms it by John's prophecy, the spirit's descent, the voice from heaven, and Jesus' successful confrontation with Satan in the desert. By the time Jesus first speaks, the reader accepts him as a reliable character and is ready to hear and trust what he says. This portrayal of Jesus as a reliable character is reinforced by the narrator's inside views, which show Jesus to be perceptive, compassionate, loving, angry at injustice or harm done to others, and anguished over his own death. By contrast, the narrator first mentions the Jewish authorities as those who teach without authority, and then presents them in opposition to the reliable protagonist. Subsequent inside views of their minds depict them watching to bring charges against Jesus, intending to test or trap him by questions, being afraid of Jesus and the crowds, and seeking to destroy Jesus out of envy. The narrator introduces the disciples favorably by means of their close association with Jesus, but later, through inside views, the narrator also shows them to be afraid, to be without understanding, as stunned and amazed, and to have hardened minds.

Thus, the narrator clearly favors some characters and not others. The introductions and inside views, along with other devices, guide the readers' perceptions of and responses to these characters.[6] The narrator's depictions explain why the reader trusts what Jesus says and does, distrusts the opponents, and has ambivalent responses to the disciples. And there is a system of values and beliefs implicit in the point of view from which the narrator judges and evaluates the characters and events in the story. This system of values and beliefs is the narrator's ideological point of view. Readers usually suspend their own values and accept the narrator's ideological assumptions—which are implicit in a story—without being aware of so doing. The reader adopts the narrator's view of the characters or events and evaluates them as the narrator does.[7]

The narrator controls distance. The narrator establishes a relationship with the reader which is different from the relationship the narrator engenders between the reader and the characters, thereby guiding the reader to be distant from or to identify with the different characters.[8] For example, from the start the narrator of Mark's story establishes with the reader a relationship of confidence by divulging the secret of Jesus' identity long before it becomes known to characters in the story, for the first line is an aside to the reader revealing that Jesus is the anointed one, the son of God. This technique puts the reader on the inside, among those who know, and enables the reader to understand more than many of the characters in the drama understand. This technique is an important foundation in this story which is concerned with what is hidden and what is secret. While this inside information creates a close relationship between the reader and the narrator, it creates distance and tension between the reader (who knows Jesus' identity) and the characters (other than Jesus) who do not know. Such a situation of tension and suspense leads the reader to wonder: How will the authorities react when they find out that Jesus acts like God's choice for king? Will the disciples ever figure out who Jesus is? And what will happen when they do? Hearing Mark's story for the first time is like watching a Hitchcock film in which the viewer is aware of a threatening situation at the opening of the film, then nervously watches the unsuspecting characters in the story become aware for themselves. In later asides, the narrator tells the reader that the Pharisees are plotting to destroy Jesus and that the disciples' minds are hardened; in both cases Jesus himself is not yet aware of these things. Again the reader is in the narrator's confidence but in tension with the unsuspecting protagonist and in suspense about the outcome.

In the examples just cited the narrator controls the reader's responses by revealing information through asides before certain characters know it. Elsewhere the narrator withholds important information from the reader so that the reader learns it at the same time some of the characters do, through the dialogue. For example, the reader learns from Jesus at the same time the disciples do that anyone who wants to follow Jesus will have to lose his life, that the rule of God is coming in power within the generation, and that the son of man will be ashamed of those who are ashamed of Jesus. Because the reader learns these threatening new developments when the disciples do, the reader tends to identify with the disciples and struggle with them in tension with Jesus over his teaching.

The narrator arranges the order of events. The narrator's employment of the events refers to the order in which the narrator introduces events into the narrative as distinct from the chronological order of events. A narrator may arrange a story in any order, chronologically or perhaps beginning near the story's end and recalling earlier events by flashback. Mark's narrator encourages certain responses in the reader by the ordering of events and also by making brief references in the story itself to events which have occurred or are yet to occur in the story world.[9] For example, the narrator creates suspense by telling the story in such a way as to foreshadow certain events: the disciples will become fishers for men; the bridegroom will be taken away; the Pharisees and Herodians will counsel to plot Jesus' destruction; Judas will hand him over; and what is now hidden will be revealed. In Mark's narrative the major device used to anticipate events is prophecy, especially those prophecies Jesus makes about his own or the disciples' impending fate. All these foreshadowings create suspense by leading the reader to wonder about and to anticipate coming events, eager to find out just when and how they will happen.

The technique of foreshadowing events enables the narrator to end the story in a powerful and enigmatic way. Throughout the narrative, by means of the prophecies, riddles, and warnings of Jesus, the narrator anticipates for the reader the future of the story world after the plotted events end. Because the reader already has some clues about the future of the story world, the narrator is able to end the story abruptly, with the women running away from the grave, afraid and saying nothing to anyone.

By means of retrospection the narrator also leads the reader to look back over the story and to reconsider earlier events in the narrative. For example, Jesus' riddle about the strong man suggests that Jesus has already bound Satan. The reader reconsiders events which have occurred in the story and comes to appreciate more fully the meaning of Jesus' confrontation with Satan in the desert. On another occasion, Jesus tells the disciples they have been given the mystery of the rule of God, and the reader reconsiders the meaning of the disciples' amazing capacity to respond to Jesus when he first called them. There are other retrospects: the flashback of John's death recalls his earlier arrest; the statements about people viewing Jesus as Elijah or as a prophet lead the reader to reconsider incidents with the crowds; the disciples' frightened response to Jesus' walking on the sea in the second boat scene is the result of their earlier failure to understand the feedings in the desert. These flashbacks or retrospects often resolve suspense by showing the outcome of what was previously foreshadowed or by clarifying some earlier enigmatic event.

POINT OF VIEW AND STANDARDS OF JUDGMENT

Point of view is a feature of narrative inextricably linked with the narrator.[10] We have already shown how the narrative reveals various aspects of the narrator's point of view. In the course of telling the story, the narrator in turn discloses the point of view of each character. "Point of view" in a narrative is expressed on four planes: the ideological system of values and beliefs of the narrator and each of the characters; the characteristic style of speech which identifies a speaker; the physical place or point in time from which a narrator or character views something; and the mental actions or emotional states of mind such as thinking, feeling, or experiencing.

Using these distinctions to analyze point of view in Mark's narrative yields many insights. We can more clearly distinguish the narrator's perspective from that of the different characters, enabling us to reconstruct the narrator and the portrayal of each character more accurately. Furthermore, we can see how the points of view of the various characters are encompassed within the overarching, consistent point of view of the narrator, who, as the storyteller, relates and often assesses the points of view of the characters. The narrator guides the reader through the narrative, showing what the authorities "think" about Jesus or what Jesus "says" about the authorities or how Jesus "sees" the faith of the cripple or how the disciples are "afraid." The narrator presents the points of view of the characters and at the same time guides the reader's evaluation of them; for example, the narrator may present the emotional point of view of the disciples, such as fear, but convey it unsympathetically from an ideological point of view which treats fear as an inappropriate response.[11]

To reconstruct the ideological points of view in a narrative is revealing. In addition to the narrator, each character has an ideological point of view that can be reconstructed from clues in the story. Among the characters of the Markan story world there consistently seem to be only two basic ideological points of view—two mentalities—represented: "thinking the things of God," evident in Jesus and most minor characters, and "thinking the things of men," reflected by the opponents of Jesus.[12] The disciples vacillate between the two points of view. The tightness and consistency of the Markan narrative in this regard is really quite extraordinary: the protagonist Jesus establishes the values, attitudes, and actions involved in thinking the things of God, and the characters either exemplify that teaching or they illustrate the contrary. In order to appreciate these two basic ideological points of view more fully, we can analyze the words, values, attitudes, beliefs, and actions of the various characters.

We can also determine the ideological point of view of the narrator. Because the narrator establishes Jesus as a reliable character, the values and attitudes of Jesus also convey those of the narrator. In addition, we can glean the narrator's point of view from the narrator's asides, commentary, explanations, manner of describing characters and events, literary techniques, view of "the writings" as authoritative, and the establishment of other characters as reliable or unreliable. The Markan narrator's ideology is consistently that of "thinking the things of God."[13] The narrator's ideological point of view, or system of values and beliefs, represents the *standards of judgment* in the story, the overarching standards by which the reader is led to evaluate and judge all subordinate points of view (those of the characters) in the story.[14]

STYLE

Style is integral to the rhetoric of a story.[15] But how, we ask, does the style of a story, as one aspect of how the story is told, affect the reader's experience of the story? We are keeping this question before us as we look at the style, the narrative patterns, and the literary techniques the narrator uses to tell this story.[16]

Mark's style is terse. Words are concrete rather than abstract. Descriptions such as "dressed in camel's hair" or "with wild animals" or "like a dove" are pictorial and suggestive, rather than detailed and exhaustive. With a few carefully chosen words, the narrator suggests things and encourages readers to use imagination.

The Rhetoric

The narrative moves along quickly, and is a lively representation of action, with little summary. The narrator "shows" the action directly, seldom talking about it indirectly. Episodes are usually brief, the scene changes often, and minor characters appear and then quickly disappear. The presence of participles, as well as a frequent occurrence of "and" and "immediately," reinforce the rapid movement of action and characters. The reader is drawn quickly into the story by means of this fast-paced, dramatic movement. The brevity of style and rapidity of motion give the narrative a tone of urgency. Thus, through the style of the narrative, the reader experiences the urgency which the protagonist conveys by his central message: The right time is fulfilled, and the rule of God has come near.

The rapid movement of action and dialogue is broken only occasionally in the story, most obviously when Jesus tells a series of riddles and later when he prophesies on the Mountain of the Olives. Otherwise it is a story of action, not discourse. As the story progresses, the frequency of the word "immediately" drops off, but reappears later to reinforce how quickly the arrest and trial of Jesus take place. And the tempo varies. Whereas early in the narrative the action shifts rapidly from one location to another, the end of the journey slows to a day-by-day description of what happens in a single location, Jerusalem, and then an hour-by-hour depiction of the crucifixion.[17] Because the whole narrative moves toward Jerusalem and toward crucifixion, the slowing of the tempo greatly intensifies the experience of this event for the reader.

NARRATIVE PATTERNS

Because of the uniqueness of every narrative, the reader cannot anticipate what narrative patterns will be part of the style of a story. They can only be open to narrative patterns which emerge in the course of reading and rereading.[18] Some of the most interesting aspects of Mark's narrative are the rhetorical devices through which the narrator orders and weaves the tale. Among these are the repetition of words, the two-step progression, the use of questions in the dialogue, the framing of one episode by another, the arrangement of episodes in a concentric pattern, and the repetition of similar episodes in a series of three.

Repetition. Mark repeats certain words and phrases, a characteristic technique of oral narration. Sometimes, the repetition occurs within episodes. For example, the narrator repeats "toll collectors and sinners" in the following section:

And many toll collectors and sinners were reclining to eat with Jesus. . . . And when the legal experts of the Pharisees saw that he was eating with the sinners and toll collectors, they said to his disciples, "Why is he eating with the toll collectors and sinners?"

Such repetition occurs within episodes in various ways: words in a question are repeated in the answer; the words in commands or requests are repeated in the descriptions of their fulfillment; a character may quote the writings and repeat key words in commenting on them; or the description of a situation or problem may be echoed in the reaction to it. This repetition alerts the reader to major themes in an episode, and its recurrence keeps the motif before the reader.[19]

Repetition of words or phrases also bridges many episodes. The choice of words throughout the story is simple and limited, yet the many key words which recur throughout the story are like major and minor motifs running through a musical composition. They are verbal threads, which weave their way through the story, giving the fabric of the story an intricate design and unity it would not otherwise have. In the first several paragraphs alone many significant verbal threads are introduced: "good news," "anointed one," "son of God," "desert," "proclaiming," "pardon," "ripped open," "tested," "handed over," "the right time," "the rule of God," "faith," "follow," "authority," and so on. Further motifs are regularly introduced in the course of the story, often signaling developments in the plot. Such verbal repetition occurs most often in epithets, actions of characters and their emotional responses, prophecies and their later fulfillment, recollections of earlier events, and the identification of settings.[20]

Such repetition provides emphasis for themes and gives continuity to the story. The repetition of a limited number of words through the many episodes provides echoes which invite the reader to make connections between one part of the narrative and another. For example, the "ripping" of the temple curtain just before the centurion recognizes Jesus as son of God recalls by verbal association the "ripping" of the heavens just before God pronounces Jesus to be his son. (Note also how the High Priest tears his vestment after Jesus' confession.) Tracing such verbal motifs through the story is illuminating. And as the words recur in similar or different contexts, they are enriched by repetition and accumulate many nuances of meaning for the reader.[21]

Two-step progression. The two-step progression is the most pervasive stylistic feature in the gospel.[22] It occurs in phrases, sentences, pairs of sentences, and the structure of episodes. It is a key to understanding many lines and episodes. A simple example is, "When it was evening, after the sun set. . . ." The time reference, "When it was evening," is repeated in "after the sun set." However, this is no mere repetition, for the second part adds precision and clarifies the first part. Both parts comprise a two-step progressive description. The first part is important, yet the emphasis often lies on the second step, which usually contains the more significant element. In this example, the second step refers to the setting sun, which denoted precisely the end of the Sabbath when people were again permitted to travel and could therefore seek out Jesus for healing. Another example is "outside, in desert places." Again, this place description is repetitious, but the second part is more precise and identifies a setting important to the story.

In addition to numerous time and place progressions, there are two-step descriptions of people and objects, such as the woman who was "Greek, a Syrophoenician by birth" and the widow who gave "everything she had, her whole living." Some parallel clauses constitute two-step progressions; for example, "the leprosy went away from him, and he was made clean" and "the right time is fulfilled, and the rule of God has come near." In antithetical parallelism, a first negative step is followed by a second and more precise step in the affirmative, such as "won't obtain a pardon ever, but is guilty of an eternal sin" or "came not to be served, but to serve and give his life." A variation of antithetical parallelism includes a general, negative statement in tandem with a qualifying exception: "This kind it isn't possible for anyone to drive out, except by prayer" and "no one is good, except the one God." Numerous pairs of questions in the dialogue signal two-step progressions, such as "What is this? A new teaching with authority?" and "Why are you cowards? Don't you have faith yet?" Progressive pairs of imperatives also occur: "Don't be afraid. Only have faith" and "Keep watch, and pray that you don't come to a testing." The two-step pattern also appears where direct discourse is preceded by a qualifying verb, the first step being a verb or verbal phrase which characterizes generally the statement of the speaker while the second step specifies precisely the actual statement. Examples include "He rebuked it, saying 'Shut up and come out from him'" and "He began teaching, and said to them, 'Isn't it written that my house shall be called a house of prayer?'"

The two-step progressions also determine the structure or movement of some episodes, especially dialogues.[23] The disciples ask Jesus two-step questions: "Tell us, when will these things be? And what will the sign be when these things are all about to be brought to an end?" Jesus responds with a lengthy two-step answer addressing each question in turn. Compare also Jesus' answers to the two-step question asked by the authorities about eating bread with defiled hands and his later answers to their progressive pair of questions about the source of Jesus' authority. Other episodes assume a two-step progressive movement from a general to a specific setting: Jesus goes to Capernaum, then to the synagogue; and he goes into Jerusalem, then into the temple. In other episodes the movement from a public to a private setting corresponds to a progression from Jesus' public teaching or action to his private explanation and clarification to the disciples.

The story of the blind man (who is touched twice to be healed) is a paradigm of how the two-step progression works for the reader. Jesus touches him once and the blind man sees, but not clearly. When Jesus touches him a second time, the blind man sees everything clearly. Similarly, the two-step progressions guide the reader to take a second look, which clarifies and emphasizes. These progressions lead the reader to see themes and emphases and to discern the structure of many episodes. They also create suspense by maintaining the reader's desire to see what is yet to come; the reader becomes conditioned to wait for the second step, for the other shoe to fall. This progression assumes importance in light of the crucial emphasis or clarification so often present in the second step.

In this regard, the overall framework of the story is the most important two-step progression. The superscription refers to Jesus as "the anointed one, the son of God." At the end of the first half of the story, Peter acknowledges Jesus as "the anointed one" and at the end of Jesus' life the centurion identifies Jesus as "son of God." The first half of the gospel emphasizes the authority of Jesus to do acts of power. The second half emphasizes the suffering of Jesus in filial obedience to God. Although the characterization of Jesus is consistent throughout, there appears, nevertheless, a clear development in the portrayal of Jesus from one half of the gospel to the next. In the first step, he serves with power; in the second, he serves as the one who suffers. Throughout the style and the structure of episodes the two-step progressions prepare the reader to be drawn more readily into seeing this larger second step and accepting this clearer, more precise understanding of Jesus.

Questions. Within this brief story, the characters pose an extraordinary number of questions, mostly rhetorical, that is, questions for which no answer is expected or only one answer could be considered correct. In Mark's story, questions heighten the drama by creating suspense and tension for the reader. Because the interrogative mood intensifies conflicts between the characters, the reader becomes absorbed in the narrative, awaiting answers to the questions and resolutions to the conflicts. The questions also reveal character.

Jesus directs many rhetorical questions to his disciples. Most commonly he hurls rhetorical questions in pairs, revealing his surprise and frustration at the disciples' failures: "Why are you cowards? Don't you have faith yet?"; "How long am I to be with you? How long am I to put up with you?"; "Simon, are you sleeping? Weren't you strong enough to keep watch one hour?" Because the questions are left unanswered, they intensify Jesus' conflict with the disciples and leave it unresolved for the reader.

Jesus most often addresses the authorities with a rhetorical question followed by an assertion in which he himself gives the obvious answer,[24] for example, "Are the attendants of the bridegroom able to fast while the bridegroom is with them? As long as they have the bridegroom with them they aren't able to fast." Or "Why does this generation seek a sign? I swear to you, surely a sign won't be given to this generation." There may be a pair of questions, or a single question with two parts, or a question and an assertion followed by another question and an assertion, or a rhetorical question followed by an action of healing which serves as the answer. In a few instances, Jesus turns a question from the opponents back to them with another question which he expects them to answer. When they do answer (sometimes they do not), Jesus then makes an assertion that answers his own question from a different point of view. This use of rhetorical questions to address the authorities enhances for the reader Jesus' authority as the one who knows, and it implies ignorance on the part of the authorities. It also creates suspense by leaving the conflict with authorities unresolved, since their defeat in debate only makes them turn more avidly against Jesus.

The questions posed by the disciples, which comprise most of their dialogue, are single questions asking Jesus to explain something. Predominant in this direct discourse are single rhetorical questions which show the disciples disbelief at what Jesus has said or done: "Surely we're not to go off and buy two hundred denarii worth of bread and give it to them to eat?" "How will anyone be able to satisfy these people with bread here in a desert?" For the reader, these questions tend to reveal the disciples' lack of understanding and faith as they are overwhelmed by Jesus' actions and his expectations of them. However, insofar as the readers are posing similar questions for themselves in reaction to events of the story, the questions encourage the readers' identification with the disciples.

When the authorities address Jesus, they do so most often with questions, usually questions posed to elicit Jesus' views on some legal matter of dispute. The opponents' questions usually convey implicit accusations, such as "Why are they [the disciples] doing what is not legal on the Sabbath?" The authorities pose various questions so as to test, trap, or secure grounds for an indictment, such as "Is it legal to give a tribute payment to Caesar or not?" In most questions the authorities reveal their hostility toward Jesus and thereby increase for the reader the tension in their conflict with Jesus.

The opponents pose very few rhetorical questions. On two significant occasions, however, opponents offer two rhetorical questions in conjunction with assertions: the very first and the very last questions asked by the Jewish authorities. The first time the authorities confront Jesus they ask in their minds, "Why does this man talk like this? He blasphemes! Who is able to pardon sins except the one God?" And at Jesus' trial, the High Priest asks, "What further need have we for witnesses? You heard the blasphemy! How does it appear to you?" In both passages, the middle sentence emphasizes the charge of blasphemy leading to Jesus' conviction.

The questions, particularly rhetorical ones, involve readers by leading them to answer the questions for themselves or to want to know how they will be answered in the story.

Framing. In some films, a scene will change in the middle of the action, leaving the viewer in suspense as to how it will turn out, while the camera shifts to another important episode of the story. Later the camera returns to continue or resolve the action begun in the initial scene. Such a framing technique occurs frequently in Mark's story.[25]

The framing device creates suspense. After being told that Jairus's daughter is near death, the reader must wait while Jesus heals the woman with the flow of blood before finding out what happens to the little girl. When the family of Jesus comes to seize him, we are left in suspense while Jesus argues with the authorities. After Peter sits down with soldiers in the courtyard of the High Priest, Jesus' trial begins before we learn what happens to Peter. Such suspense maintains the reader's interest, enticing him or her to pay attention to the future direction of the story.

This framing also provides commentary. The two related stories illuminate and enrich each other, commenting on and clarifying the meaning, one of the other. This is sometimes done by comparison: Jesus' family thinking he is crazy is comparable to the legal experts saying he is possessed; the faith of Jairus for his daughter is comparable to the faith of the woman for her own healing; and Jesus' cursing of the fig tree which has no fruit parallels his attack on the temple authorities for failing to administer the temple properly. At other times, the framing provides commentary by contrast: sending disciples out with no food contrasts sharply with Herod's banquet, and Peter's denial of Jesus illuminates, by contrast, Jesus' courageous confession at his trial. Details of these comparisons and contrasts highlight major themes of the gospel: the blindness of those on the "outside," the power of faith, judgment on Israel, testifying in the face of death, and so on.

Episodes in concentric patterns. Mark also occasionally arranges episodes in a concentric pattern, a common technique of ancient narration.[26] In the concentric pattern, episodes are not interrupted as with framing. Rather, related episodes form rings around one central episode. A comparison of the paired episodes illuminates and enriches many aspects of these stories.

The five conflicts between Jesus and the authorities in Galilee show a concentric relationship of A, B, C, B^1, and A^1. Paired episodes A and A^1 along with B and B^1 form an outer and an inner ring around the central episode C. Episode A (the healing of the cripple) and episode A^1 (the healing of the withered hand) reflect each other in structure, content, and theme: both occur indoors, involve the healing of the body, and include the same characters (Jesus, the authorities, and the person healed); both healings are delayed while the narrator reveals unspoken accusations against Jesus (blasphemy in A and healing on the Sabbath in A^1); and both involve serious legal penalties. Furthermore, in both episodes Jesus responds to the unspoken accusations with rhetorical questions. Cleverly he avoids indictment by healing instead of pardoning sins (thus avoiding the charge of blasphemy) in episode A, and by not touching the withered hand (thus avoiding the charge of doing work on the Sabbath) in episode A^1.

Episodes B (eating with the sinners) and B^1 (picking grain on the Sabbath) are also related: both are concerned with eating and with uncleanness (from toll collectors in B and from violation of the Sabbath in B^1). The form of both episodes includes an action, the authorities' objections and Jesus' explanation of the action. Both involve the same characters (Jesus, disciples, and the authorities). In both cases, Jesus answers with a proverb and then with a statement of his purpose and authority.

These four episodes (A, B, B^1, A^1) form two concentric patterns around episode C in which Jesus teaches about fasting (in contrast to the eating theme of B and B^1). By contrast with other episodes, the setting is indefinite and the questioners are not specified. Nor are the questioners hostile. As a result, this central episode focuses on Jesus' response rather than on conflicts or actions, and Jesus' response illuminates all five of the episodes that make up the concentric pattern. His reference to the bridegroom being "taken away" points to the possible consequences of opposition by the authorities in A and A^1, the death penalty for blasphemy or for breaking the Sabbath. And Jesus' reference to putting new wine in old wineskins shows how the authorities use old categories of law and tradition to judge the newness Jesus represents (and both the wine and the wineskins will be destroyed). Also, the series thematically contrasts Jesus' authority with that of the Jewish leaders. Jesus has authority to pardon sins (A) and eats with sinners (B). He is special like a bridegroom or something new (C). He has authority over the Sabbath (B^1) and heals on the Sabbath (A^1).[27] By contrast, the Jewish leaders have authority only to accuse, and they fail to get an indictment.

These five "conflict" episodes create a dramatic experience for the reader. One clash is followed by a second, then a third which clarifies the first two. With this clarification in mind, the reader experiences another conflict which recalls the second episode and then a final clash which recalls the first episode. The characters, actions, and dialogue in each episode illuminate the other episodes by comparison and association. This particular circular pattern also contains a linear progression. From the first to the fifth episodes, Jesus' frustration grows as he futilely tries to explain his actions. Also, the opposition of the authorities gradually escalates and intensifies. For the reader, this linear progression combines with the circular progression to heighten the tension and to form a climax in the final episode: the linear pattern culminates in the Pharisees trying to get charges against Jesus and the concentric pattern returns to the serious death threat implicit in the first story. At the end of the series, the entire conflict is propelled forward when the Pharisees go out to plot with the Herodians as to "how they might destroy him."

The other major example of the concentric pattern in Mark's story is the series of Jesus' conflicts with the authorities in Jerusalem, comprised of seven episodes: Episodes A and A^1 involve Jesus' statement of judgment against the authorities (the riddle of the wicked tenants and the warning against the scribes). Episodes B and B^1 include a quotation from the psalms followed by a reaction to that citation (the quotations about the cornerstone and David's son); and episodes C and C^1 are both legal discussions about love for God and neighbor (Caesar and God, and love for God and neighbor). Episode D is the central episode; its topic is the resurrection, and its theme illuminates all the episodes: the failure of the authorities to understand either the writings or the power of God. In contrast to the series of debates in Galilee, the linear progression in these episodes moves toward a gradual lessening of verbal opposition to Jesus. Jesus' triumph in debate reinforces the rightness of his own interpretation of the legal and other writings, and exposes the absence of legal grounds for the subsequent arrest of Jesus by the authorities.

Episodes in a series of three. Perhaps the most commonly recognized pattern of narration in Mark is the threefold repetition of similar actions and events. Criteria for the identification of these series of three have included the repetition of narrative structure, verbal threads, a common theme, the continuation of a conflict, the involvement of the same characters, and the similarity of setting. Some series are obvious because they occur in direct sequence: at Gethsemane, Jesus returns from prayer three times to find the disciples sleeping;[28] Peter denies Jesus three times; Pilate asks the crowd three leading questions, each of which is rejected; and the narrator recounts events of the crucifixion at three, three-hour intervals (nine o'clock, noon, and three o'clock).[29]

Other series of three occur at intervals. For example, during the journey to Jerusalem, Jesus predicts his death three times.[30] After each prediction, the disciples' response indicates that they do not understand. After each response, Jesus summons the disciples and teaches them the values of the rule of God implicit in his predictions. In an earlier series, Jesus makes the disciples fishers of men: in the first episode, he calls four fishermen to follow him; in the second, he makes the twelve; and in the third, he sends them out to proclaim and heal.[31] Also, there are three similar scenes of conflict between Jesus and his disciples in a boat and three progressive episodes of conflict between Jesus and his disciples in which bread is the center of discussion and action.[32] These two series are especially dramatic since the third bread scene coincides with the third conflict in the boat. And on three successive days, Jesus enters the temple in Jerusalem: the first time to look around, the second time to attack and briefly occupy it, and the third time to predict its destruction.[33]

This threefold pattern of narration underscores the definitive failure of the disciples. When Jesus asks the disciples to stay awake and they fall asleep once, perhaps the reader may excuse them. When Jesus finds them sleeping a second time, there may still be room for doubt. But when Jesus finds them sleeping a third time, the reader knows the definitive extent to which the disciples have failed Jesus. The boat incidents, the bread scenes, the resistance to Jesus' three predictions, and Peter's denial effect a similar impression. This series maintains the reader's interest in the fate of the disciples in the story. Also, a threefold series is no mere repetition of similar events, but involves a progressive development. Each incident uncovers more about the characters or the conflicts, and the third episode fully reveals the dynamic of that entire series: for example, the third bread scene exposes dramatically the blindness of the disciples and the extent of their conflict with Jesus already made evident in the first two bread scenes. The series thus creates suspense for the reader, who comes to anticipate a buildup to a dramatic climax. The reader is thereby prepared to view the three episodes of a series in relation to each other. That is, when the series unfolds, the reader then looks back from the perspective of the third scene and understands more clearly the issues involved in the first and second scenes.[34]

OTHER LITERARY FEATURES

There are other literary-rhetorical features of Mark's narrative which are significant for interpretation: the riddles, the quotations from the writings, the prophetic oracles, and irony.

Riddles. Often in literature a character tells a strange story or recounts an obscure dream. The interpretation of the story may not be immediately clear, but the reader perceives some clue to the meaning of events in the story contained in it. Mark's gospel has many such "stories within a story." The protagonist Jesus tells cryptic stories and makes obscure statements. These stories and statements are commonly referred to as parables, but because of their peculiar use in Mark's gospel, it is more appropriate to refer to them as riddles. As riddles they must be deciphered by other characters in the story (and by the reader) in order for their meaning to be disclosed.[35] Once deciphered, the riddles appear to be allegories about the hidden presence of the rule of God in the story world; that is, they are cryptic stories about a hidden reality. Depending on who hears them, the riddles will reveal or obscure. Jesus assumes that for someone who already perceives the mystery of the hidden rule of God the riddles will further clarify that rule, but for someone who does not understand the mystery of the rule of God the riddles will only obscure matters further.

The riddles are allegories that Jesus tells which interpret Jesus, events, and people in the story world as part of the rule of God. This function becomes apparent when we look at the four riddles which Jesus explains to the disciples. Jesus interprets the riddle of the sower as an allegory about those responding to the proclamation of the rule of God. The sower is the one who proclaims (above all, Jesus) and the seed is the word. Elements of the riddle correlate with various characters in the story, the ways they respond to the word and the final outcome of the rule of God. The riddle about defilement explains, through allegory, that the unclean food which the disciples eat will not defile them, but that evil plans and actions *will* defile people. The riddle about the fig tree is an allegory about how the disciples are to discern the signs that will accompany the final establishment of the rule of God. And the riddle about the man who went away and told the doorkeeper to keep watch further allegorizes how Jesus will be absent after his death and the disciples (and others) are to prepare for his return. Thus, the riddles are allegories about aspects of the rule of God as manifest in events of the story world.

By so understanding riddles it is possible to clarify other riddles which Jesus does not explain. For example, to the opponents Jesus relates the allegorical riddle about the strong man in order to explain his exorcisms. The two brief riddles about secrets being revealed affirm that the present hiddenness of God's rule and the secret of Jesus' identity will eventually come to light. The riddle about the seed growing secretly and the riddle about the mustard seed allegorize the faith of the sower, the assured growth of the seed, and the overwhelming outcome. The riddle of the vineyard interprets events in light of God's relation to Israel in the story, including the reason God sends a son, the causes and consequences of his death, and the ultimate fate of the opponents and the vineyard. Other sayings may also be riddles, although they are not designated as such: the sayings about the bridegroom, the wine and wineskins, the children's bread for the dogs, and salting with fire.

Jesus addresses the riddles to the characters in the story. He tells riddles to be understood by those who "have ears to hear," for he prefaces some riddles with commands to "Hear! Look!" and "Look at what you hear" and "Hear me everyone and understand." Jesus assumes that the disciples and those around him will be able to understand the riddles, because they "have been given the mystery of the rule of God" (that is, because they have discerned that the hidden rule of God is present in Jesus), as evidenced by their having left everything and followed him. Jesus assumes that the disciples will be able to decipher the allegorical riddles and learn from them. He is surprised when the disciples do not understand the riddles, so he unravels their meaning for them. When it is obvious later that they have still not understood them, he becomes angry.

On the other hand, Jesus tells the riddles in order that those on the outside will *not* understand, "so that looking they look, and don't see, and hearing they hear, and don't understand. Otherwise they might turn and be pardoned." At the point in the story when Jesus states his reason for telling riddles, the authorities have already rejected Jesus and committed the "eternal sin" of claiming that he is possessed. They are clearly on the outside, blind and deaf to the rule of God. Jesus intends that for those who have not been given the mystery of the rule of God—who do not perceive God's hidden rule in Jesus—the riddles will obscure matters further.

Also, Jesus' riddles sometimes enable him to avoid arrest. Because of opposition by the authorities, Jesus cannot always speak plainly to them without risking indictment. By explaining his exorcisms with a riddle, Jesus avoids a charge of blasphemy. The riddle about defiled food, which implies a contravention of written laws, and the riddle about the source of Jesus' authority also enable Jesus to state his message in cryptic terms which do not expose him to indictment.

What is the effect of a story with riddles? In part, the riddles make the story intriguing by offering enigmas for the reader to decipher. The reader, who overhears these riddles, is in a better position to understand the riddles than the characters are, since from the outset the reader knows Jesus' identity and his relation to the rule of God. Understanding the riddles enables the reader to understand better the meaning of those events in the story to which the allegorical riddles refer. This understanding in turn increases the reader's alignment with the world views of Jesus and the narrator, and it creates distance from the characters who do not understand. On the other hand, the riddles may be enigmatic and cryptic to the readers also, leading them to wonder whether they understand any better than the disciples do. This effect involves the readers further in the story in order to gain insights which will make them feel on the inside rather than on the outside of understanding.

Quotations from the writings. In J. D. Salinger's *Franny and Zooey,* the older brother Seymour, whom the rest of the family seeks to emulate, lists quotations from various religious and philosophical writings on the back of his bedroom door. These quotations provide clues to unlock the meaning of Salinger's story. Other literature yields similar examples—a character cites a passage from some well-known book or quotes a famous person from the past. Such references are never incidental. They are pieces of the puzzle a reader puts together to interpret a story. In Mark's gospel, there are twenty-two quotations from "the writings," which include the Law (now the first five books of the Hebrew Bible), the Psalms, and the Prophets, all held in common as scriptures by the Jewish characters in the story.[36] There are many minor allusions and several paraphrases (following the introduction "it is necessary"), but our concern here is with the obvious quotations. In our translation, these quotes have been set off in parallel poetic lines or explicitly identified as quotations by the characters who cite them.

It is significant that all but two of the quotations occur in dialogue. Only Jesus and the authorities quote the writings. The quotations reveal the characters who quote them. Those quotations which occur in legal debate reveal, on the one hand, the superior knowledge and authority of Jesus and, on the other hand, the ignorance and blindness of the authorities, who are supposed to be "legal experts" in the writings. Also, Jesus establishes his authority in part by citing prophecies which come to be fulfilled. Apart from quotations in the dialogue, the narrator cites the writings twice: in the opening prophecy (an aside) and in the description of those who cast lots for Jesus' clothes.

In addition to revealing character, the citations from the writings, like the riddles, interpret the significance of characters and events in relation to the plan and rule of God. Quotations from the writings explain the origin of John's baptism, the hypocrisy of the Pharisees, the purpose of the riddles, the stumbling of the disciples, God's plan for the execution of Jesus, and so on. Jesus cites these writings as both explanation and interpretation of events for other characters, but their presence in the story serves the same function for the readers, who "overhear" them.

Prophecies. There are many prophetic oracles in the story, some cited from the writings and others given by characters in the story, namely John and Jesus. Some of these prophecies are fulfilled in the narrative, but not in any mechanistic way; rather, the story portrays realistically the integrity and motives of the characters to whom the prophecies refer. Jesus knows that according to prophecy it is God's plan for him to suffer, yet his own character is realized only as he struggles to be obedient. Jesus recalls for the authorities an oracle about a stone which "the builders" will reject, yet it is precisely their anger with Jesus for citing the oracle against them which in part leads them to carry out the very act which fulfills the oracle. Jesus then relates to the disciples an oracle which prophesies that they will be scattered when the shepherd is struck, yet it is their false confidence that this will never happen to them which leads the disciples to be unprepared for testing when it comes. For the reader, these prophetic oracles increase the pathos of the characters' struggle with their destiny. They also lure the reader into identifying sympathetically with Jesus and the disciples.

All the prophecies together have a significant impact on the reader. There are the prophetic oracles cited from the writings, some of which are fulfilled in the narrative and some of which will be fulfilled in the future of the story world. Other oracles originate from characters in the story, first John and then Jesus. Some of Jesus' oracles, those related to his death and resurrection, are fulfilled in the narrative, and others will be fulfilled in the future of the story world. The reader is encouraged from the first few lines to expect the prophetic oracles to be fulfilled. The prophecies foreshadow events, and the descriptions of those events are often structured so as to demonstrate how they fulfill the prophecies. Because so many prophecies of Jesus are fulfilled in the narrative, the reader comes to trust that the prophecies about the future story world and the final establishment of the rule of God in a generation would also be fulfilled just as prophesied. Also, because all oracles are related to the plan and rule of God, the reader experiences how the establishment of that rule over the world provides the larger framework of the story world, the past and the future, including the impetus and goal of the narrated events.

Irony. Irony is a dominant feature of Mark's story.[37] *Verbal irony* occurs when a speaker self-consciously says one thing but means the opposite. *Situational irony* occurs when there is a discrepancy between what a character naively expects to happen and what actually happens, or between what a character blindly thinks to be the case and what the real situation is.

The most obvious examples of verbal irony in Mark are the ironic jeers of Jesus' opponents. The soldiers "mock" him by hailing him "king of the Jews," putting a thorn crown on his head, and striking him with a reed staff. They mean the opposite: how ridiculous that this pathetic man should be considered a king. Others taunt him to prophesy or to get off the cross or to tear down the temple; they command him to do amazing, impossible things, but sarcastically they mean the opposite: how helpless and incapable he is, hardly the anointed one of God!

In situational irony the speaker is confident that what he or she says or expects is true, but is unaware that the real situation is, in fact, the opposite. The characters in the story are blind victims of the irony of the situation, while the reader sees the ironic contrast between what the speaker says and the way things really are. For example, when the opponents ridicule Jesus for claiming to be king of the Jews, the reader sees that the statements which they intend to be ironic sarcasm really are true: Jesus can prophesy; he really is king of the Jews; his death will secure the destruction of the temple;[38] and he cannot save himself except by losing his life. Also, the disciples are often in the center of ironic situations. Peter vehemently insists that he will die with Jesus rather than deny him. But the reader knows the real situation is other-wise, because Jesus has just prophesied that Peter will renounce him three times. Furthermore, Peter's name, "Rock," is ironic, for he thinks he is like a rock. He happens to be the opposite of what his nick-name suggests, for he falls asleep and later falls apart under the incriminating remarks of a maid of the High Priest.

In the larger design of the gospel, the situational irony predominates. This irony roots itself in the nature of the rule of God as differentiated from what most characters in the story expect. For example, the authorities expect the rule of God to affirm their own authority and interpretation of the law, when in fact God has given authority to Jesus the Nazarene who interprets the law quite differently. The authorities expect the rule of God to be established openly with Elijah coming first to set everything right, but the real situation is that the rule first comes in hiddenness and the agents of it are to suffer and die. The authorities expect those who were most important now to be first also in the rule of God (those greatest in human eyes would be greatest in the rule of God), but the values of the rule of God are the reverse of their expectations. The contrast between the opponents' expectations and what is really happening comes to a climax at the trial: the opponents think they have rightly condemned this blasphemer to death, when in fact *they* are the blasphemers who have opposed God's rule and God's agent and who have sealed their own doom.

The disciples also participate in the larger irony of the story. They follow Jesus to become fishers for men, but his way leads them to death. They expect to gain glory, wealth, and power from their association with this anointed agent of God's rule. What they gain instead is an invitation to be a slave to everyone and suffer death. They expect one thing; they encounter the opposite.

Ironic contrasts structure the story. The rule of God is hidden; the identity of the anointed one is secret; those disciples whom Jesus thought were on the inside turn out to be blind like those on the outside; Israel's leaders are blind to the rule of God; the rule of God overturns all worldly expectations; the most important are the least; the greatest become slaves; those losing their lives are saving them; and the king rules from a cross.[39]

Irony has a way of drawing readers into accepting the narrator's point of view. By showing the authorities ridiculing Jesus, the narrator leads the reader to sympathize with Jesus and smile slyly, saying "There's more truth to that than they know." And because the reader sees what the real situation is, in contrast to the characters who do not see, the reader is led to be on the inside, perhaps even to feel superior to the blind victims of the irony.[40] The ending of Mark, however, punctures any self-confident superiority the reader might feel, for the ending turns irony back upon the reader. Throughout the story when Jesus commanded people to be quiet they talked anyway. But at the end when the young man commands the women to go tell the message—the crucial message—in an ironic reversal they are silent. The fear of the women dominates the ending of the story. At this point fear forces the reader to face once again the fear in his or her own situation. No matter how much the reader "knows" or "sees," he or she still must make the hard choice in the end—whether to be silent like the women or to proclaim the good news in the face of persecution and possible death.

Summary. The rhetoric we have discussed in this chapter can be illustrated in virtually every episode of the gospel. By recognizing these rhetorical devices, and how they function, one is able to reconstruct the elements of the story world: comprehending the narrator's role for an assessment of the characters; interpreting the riddles for the analysis of conflicts; discerning concentric structures for clarifying plot development; and so on. Because form is inseparable from the content, rhetoric from story, we appropriate these rhetorical techniques and features in order to analyze the settings, the plot, and the characters of this artful gospel.

3

The Settings

The settings of a story provide the context for the conflicts and for the actions of the characters. That context is often quite integral to the story, for settings can serve many functions essential to plot: generating atmosphere, determining conflict, revealing traits in the characters who must deal with problems or threats caused by the settings, offering commentary (sometimes ironic) on the action, and evoking associations and nuances of meaning present in the culture of the readers. Settings may even provide structure to a story, in addition to conveying important themes. Settings can be no less significant for a story than stage sets are for theater drama.[1]

We see the importance of settings if we reflect on their presence in many familiar stories: for example, the sea in Herman Melville's *Moby Dick;* the settings related to journeys in Homer's *Odyssey* and Dante's *Divine Comedy;* the path to the town in Eudora Welty's "A Worn Path"; and the wilderness in Jack London's novels. If the settings in these stories were altered, the stories themselves would be changed significantly.

In Mark's story, settings provide the overall framework for the movement and for the development of plot. The first half of the story has a setting in Galilee, the second half in Jerusalem. The whole story is a journey which begins with travel throughout Galilee, followed by a pilgrimage to Jerusalem. Themes, events, conflicts, and character roles develop and come into sharp focus as the story moves from powerful action in Galilee towards confrontation and death in Jerusalem. On the way, many local settings contribute significantly to the story and its impact: the river, the desert, the sea, mountains—as well as houses, boats, synagogues, and the temple.

The major settings in Mark's story are seldom neutral. Jesus moves in a hostile world, entering situations which are already highly charged with meaning and power. In Galilean towns he encounters violent demonic forces and antagonistic authorities. He must deal with the destruction threatened by the sea and the desert. And in the hostile atmosphere of Jerusalem, he faces overwhelming political opposition.

As a dimension of setting, the "time" is also highly charged. The Sabbath day poses the threat of indictment to Jesus. The Passover festival, a volatile celebration of nationalistic fervor, intensifies the conflicts in Jerusalem and provides a highly meaningful occasion for Jesus' death.[2] More than these, the whole story is set into motion by the declaration that "the right time is fulfilled, and the rule of God has come near." This time has long been awaited. Dramatic actions of salvation take place in this time, with an urgency required by the imminent threat and promise of the final establishment of God's rule in power.

THE "WAY"

The journey provides thematic structure to the story.[3] The opening prophecy twice refers to the "way," anticipating the journey that is to follow in the story. This prophecy gives added meaning to what follows, because it invites the reader to recall journeys in Israelite history. In Mark's story John "prepares the way" for Jesus, who then travels throughout Galilee with his disciples. Jesus travels several times into gentile territory and comes back to Galilee. He sends out his disciples, telling them to take nothing "on the way" except a walking stick.

The verbal motif of "the way" appears most often in the description of Jesus' journey to Jerusalem, which begins on the way to the villages around Caesarea Philippi in gentile territory (in the other direction from Jerusalem). The beginning of the journey to Jerusalem marks a turning point in the story: Peter acknowledges Jesus as the anointed one, and Jesus begins to teach the disciples about death. The journey moves back through Galilee to Capernaum, then to Judea and beyond the Jordan, then to Jericho and to Bethphage and Bethania at the Mountain of the Olives. The journey ends in confrontation and death in Jerusalem. (As a verbal thread, the "way" occurs eight times in the depiction of this journey, thereby providing a structure for the story.)

The journey is the way of God. Being "on the way" means more than moving through a physical landscape to Jerusalem; it also means that Jesus moves toward the goal God has set for him: death in the service of proclaiming God's rule. For the disciples, this journey is a movement toward an understanding and an acceptance of what Jesus' "way" is. The journey ends ironically in Jerusalem, when the opponents flatter Jesus hypocritically by telling him that he "truthfully teaches *the way of God*"—a statement which neither the opponents nor the disciples have grasped.

The motif of the journey is also conveyed by the verbal threads which indicate "going ahead" and "following." John is sent "ahead" of Jesus, and Jesus goes "ahead" of the disciples. Jesus comes "after" John, and the disciples "follow after" Jesus. These words are not merely temporal and spatial descriptions; they reflect the pattern of life which is "the way of God." John goes ahead of Jesus by anticipating the pattern of Jesus' life: he was sent by God, proclaimed, was handed over, and was put to death. Jesus' life is subsequently characterized by the same powerful words. And the disciples are to follow: they are sent in order to proclaim; they will be handed over; and they are to take up their crosses and lose their lives. Thus, "the way of God" anticipated by John and traveled by Jesus is to be followed by the disciples.[4]

LOCAL SETTINGS RECALLING ISRAEL'S PAST

On the journey there are many settings which recall events in Israel's history, events associated primarily with the journeys which Israel made in the desert in preparation for restoration by God. The settings provide atmosphere for the story; they also create conflicts and reveal character.[5]

The river. John baptizes at the Jordan River. The river provided a threshold experience in Israel's history. After Israel's exodus from Egypt, crossing the Jordan signalled the entrance to "the promised land." Even in the first century, Jewish prophets led followers to re-enact the crossing of the Jordan River in hopes of anticipating Israel's liberation from the Roman Empire. Mark's story opens with people coming out to be baptized at the Jordan River, preparing the way for the lord.

Desert. In this story, the desert has a hostile and threatening atmosphere; it is desolate and barren. It is important to the story as a place of preparation. John prepares there for Jesus, and Jesus is driven there to encounter Satan in preparation for his messianic role. In the opening lines of the story Isaiah's prophecy invites recollections of Israel's past.

The prophecy was originally proclaimed for people to "prepare" the way for God to lead the Israelites back across the desert from exile in Babylonia. The desert also has an association with the earlier event in Israel's history when the people wandered forty years in the desert in preparation for entering the land of Israel. Both of these journeys were associated with new beginnings. Thus, early in the story, the desert settings "prepare" the reader for the new activity of God which is to follow.

In the story the hostile desert also becomes a place of testing. Unlike the Israelites who lost faith during the forty years of wandering in the desert, Jesus successfully endures forty days of testing by Satan, and the angels serve him. Later, the desert tests the disciples, twice revealing their lack of faith.[6] Like the ancient Israelites, the disciples do not have faith that God can provide bread in such a barren place. By contrast, Jesus' faith in God enables him to provide for the crowd. God's abundant provision of bread is all the more dramatic against the harsh barrenness of the place, and once again the setting provides an association with the desert where God provided manna through Moses.[7]

Sea. In Mark's story, the sea is a place of chaos and destruction. In the dialogue the sea is a place to throw someone with a millstone tied around the neck or a place to cast a mountain to destroy it. In the events of the story, the herd of two thousand pigs and the demons possessing them are destroyed in the sea. A dramatic storm on the Sea of Galilee also threatens to destroy Jesus and the disciples. Such storm episodes invite readers to recall the chaos of the waters in Israelite creation stories and the destructiveness of the flood.

The raging sea elicits Jesus' faith and highlights the extent of his authority from God over nature: he stops the wind, calms the sea, and later walks on the sea. These episodes recall the divine authority which brought creative order out of chaos and which parted the Reed (Red) Sea. The sea also tests the disciples, revealing their lack of faith. Though experienced fishermen, the disciples are terrified of being swamped by the storm while Jesus sleeps.[8]

Mountains. The mountain is a setting of refuge and safety in this story. Jesus warns that, at the threat of war, people in Judea should "flee to

66

the mountains." Mountains also suggest closeness to God. Jesus often retreats to a mountain to pray, for example, after feeding a crowd in the desert and at Gethsemane before his arrest.

The mountain is also a setting for revelation. On a mountain glory comes upon Jesus and a voice reveals to the three disciples that Jesus is God's only son. On the Mountain of the Olives, Jesus reveals to four disciples the future of God's rule in prophecies and warnings. In Israelite history, God gave the Law to Moses on a mountain; there God was made manifest to Moses and later to Elijah. The mountain setting triggers these associations, thereby enriching the meanings of the episodes which occur there.

PRIVATE AND PUBLIC SETTINGS

Some settings create privacy for Jesus and his disciples. Jesus often retreats with the disciples to a house, a boat, or a mountain. These private settings serve several functions. They provide the context for Jesus' private teaching to his disciples, such as the explanations of riddles or prophecies of his death and resurrection or prophecies about the future. These private settings contribute to the secrecy motif of the story because those characters present, as well as the reader, have access to what goes on there, but the other characters do not. Also, by isolating Jesus with the disciples, these private settings highlight the conflicts between them. For example, the confined setting of the boat magnifies the intensity of the conflicts Jesus has with his disciples there.[9]

In addition, the private settings isolate the conflicts of Jesus with the disciples from his conflicts with the authorities. The story is set in such a way that almost all conflicts between Jesus and the disciples occur in private, whereas in public the disciples are usually aligned with Jesus, who defends their actions to the authorities. By means of the isolation of conflicts provided by the settings, the narrator leads the reader to think of the disciples as being "with" Jesus and "for" him even when they are in conflict with him.

By contrast, the conflicts between Jesus and the authorities occur in public settings where they are openly pitted against each other for all to see. These public settings contribute to the suspenseful atmosphere of the conflicts. The synagogue and temple are especially threatening places for Jesus, because they are legal centers where charges are brought and trials held. There the authorities are on their own turf. Ironically, Jesus is not so vulnerable in public because the crowds present in these public settings often protect him from arrest.

PATTERNS OF MOVEMENT

Galilee. Many local settings, when seen in relation to each other, form patterns and convey themes. One such pattern is the movement from place to place; Jesus changes setting more than forty times in his travels throughout Galilee and into gentile territory. Frequent movement suggests a hurried journey underscoring the urgency of Jesus' message. It also enhances Jesus' authority, reestablished in city after city. Travel also emphasizes the extent to which God's rule is proclaimed throughout the nation and beyond. When Peter and those with him want Jesus to return to Capernaum, he replies, "Let's go elsewhere, to the nearby towns, so I might proclaim there too, for that's why I came out." Jesus proclaims the rule of God and the travels are necessary to accomplish this purpose. Later Jesus sends his disciples out to proclaim. He tells them to travel by twos and to depend on others for their provisions, procedures which facilitate movement from one locale to the next.

The patterns in some settings throughout his travels in Galilee highlight the great popular response of the crowds to Jesus. By tracing the episodes which occur in a house, a confined setting which accentuates the developing complications due to large crowds, we can detect this pattern. First, Jesus enters the house of Simon's mother-in-law in Capernaum, and by evening the whole city is gathered at the door. When he returns to Capernaum, so many people gather that there is not even room at the door, and some people have to tear off part of the roof to reach Jesus for healing. Later, in another house, such a huge crowd gathers that Jesus and his disciples are not able to eat. Subsequently houses are no longer a setting of public activity for Jesus. This same problem with crowds recurs in towns, another confined setting. At one point the crowds are so great that Jesus is no longer even able to enter a town openly.

The popular response to Jesus is further accentuated when the crowds become a problem even in the open settings to which Jesus escapes from the problems in houses and towns. "Beside the sea" is one such setting. When Jesus first passes by the Sea of Galilee, he is alone and chooses four men to follow him. When he returns to the sea, a huge crowd follows him. Later, an even larger crowd follows him alongside the sea—a crowd comprised not only of those from Galilee but others from Judea and Jerusalem and Idumea and across the Jordan and around Tyre and Sidon. He tells his disciples to keep a little boat waiting so the crowd will not crush him. When Jesus next travels alongside the sea, the crowd is so huge that he is forced into a boat and teaches away from the shore. That evening, Jesus and his disciples avoid the crowds by going to the other side via boat. A similar pattern in the open setting of the desert also displays this popular response to Jesus.

Another pattern is noticeable when Jesus encounters complication or conflict—in almost every setting. He is not always free to journey from place to place as he pleases. He moves on not only to proclaim in other places but also to withdraw from opponents seeking to indict him, from his family's efforts to seize him, from the crowds in order to pray, or to rest from the huge crowds which flock to him. In almost all settings Jesus encounters difficulties which compel him to move on.

All these patterns suggest that the way of God which Jesus travels in Galilee is not an ordered journey from one town to the next; Jesus often moves on because of complications and conflicts which he is unable to prevent or control. When the reader experiences Jesus' rapid movement among these settings interwoven in the story, the impact is one of great turmoil and activity: Jesus moves on from Capernaum to avoid crowds and proclaim elsewhere, but then he goes out to desert places because he cannot openly enter a town, he returns to Capernaum where he encounters a crowd in the house and the menacing presence of legal experts—so he retreats to the sea where he is followed by a huge crowd, and so on. For the reader, the impact of this activity and turmoil accentuates the urgency of Jesus' efforts to proclaim, exorcise, and heal, as well as his frustrations at not being able to control these obstacles and conflicts at every turn.

Gentile Territory. Jesus travels to gentile territory, areas around Tyre and Sidon and the region of the Ten Cities across the Sea of Galilee, where he encounters gentile people such as the pig herders and the Syro-

Phoenician woman. In the culture of the time the gospel was written, Jews made a distinction between Jewish and gentile territory. Jews considered their land to be holy and the gentile land unclean. Through this depiction of Jesus as a traveller among gentiles, the narrator portrays him as open to and compassionate toward gentiles. Interestingly, the same patterns of response to Jesus in Galilee recur among gentiles: great popularity, intense opposition, withdrawal from opposition, healing and proclaiming which leads to even larger crowds, crowds in the desert, little privacy for Jesus, and Jesus' efforts to keep people quiet producing the opposite effect. The recurrence of the pattern among gentiles reveals a similar response to Jesus among both Jews and gentiles in the story world.

Journey to Jerusalem. When Jesus heads toward Jerusalem, the journey takes on purpose and direction. Gradually the reader becomes aware that Jerusalem is his destination and that his journey is a pilgrimage to Passover. The events and dialogue on the way reveal the journey primarily as an inexorable march by Jesus to his death. This determined movement toward Jerusalem heightens the suspense and the tension in anticipation of the events to take place there.

This journey also creates a funneling effect for the whole story.[10] In the first half of the story the movement ranges widely throughout Galilee and beyond. Then the direction narrows in toward Jerusalem, finally ending there. The settings of the story channel the characters, the conflicts, and the actions toward a dramatic conclusion in Jerusalem, thereby intensifying the climactic events which take place there.

THE END OF THE JOURNEY

Jerusalem and the Temple. When Jesus reaches his destination in Jerusalem, the complications he encountered earlier are magnified. Jerusalem is the capital of Israel—the heart of Judaism. The huge, magnificent temple complex, the center of authority for the high priests and legal experts, dominated the city. In the story, Jerusalem, teeming with people at the national celebration of the Passover, evokes an atmosphere of expectation and tension. The mortal conflict which takes place in Jerusalem is anticipated early in the story when legal experts and Pharisees come from Jerusalem to discredit Jesus. Jesus' prophecies of his impending trial and death also foreshadow the clash in Jerusalem. And Jesus goes to Jerusalem to bring these events about. Dramatically he enters Jerusalem as the one who comes in the Lord's name, ushering in God's rule. He attacks and occupies the temple, teaching how the temple should serve gentiles. And he takes on the authorities in debate.[11]

Just as Jesus had encountered opposition in the synagogues in Galilee, he now meets intense opposition from all the authorities. In Jerusalem Jesus is under constant threat. Yet the crowds overwhelmingly favor him and during the daytime protect him from arrest. And at night Jesus withdraws to settings outside the city. Only at the last does he enter the city at night where he has arranged secretly for the Passover meal. Then he and his disciples go to the Mountain of the Olives. Earlier the mountain setting was a place where Jesus avoided the crowds and the opposition. Now, while he prays, a hostile crowd from the authorities arrives with swords and clubs to arrest him. And here, at the end, the pattern we have seen in other settings is reversed; the opposition triumphs. The crowds no longer follow Jesus or protect him but are manipulated against him by the authorities. Jerusalem, the capital of Israel, the place where God dwells in the temple, is the place where Jesus is rejected and killed. Yet here in this place, his death is also his enthronement as God's king.

The final scene points back to Galilee, back to the beginning of the story. The young man's message at the tomb with instructions for the disciples to go to Galilee suggests perhaps a fresh start for the disciples or for anyone in the future of the story world who chooses to follow Jesus. By implication, this fresh journey will result in the same complications and the same hostility met in Galilee by John and then by Jesus. Furthermore, Galilee points away from Jerusalem, the center of Judaism, toward gentile nations, where Jesus had said the good news was to be proclaimed before the end came.[12] According to prophecies in the story, the disciples will not receive any different treatment from the authorities in a gentile setting than they received from authorities in Galilee or Jerusalem, for Jesus prophesied that they will stand trial before gentile governors and kings, just as they will be handed over to Jewish sanhedrins and will be beaten in synagogues. As with Jesus, the way of God for others will lead them to settings of confrontation and rejection.

SUMMARY

Settings are integral to this story in a variety of ways. Even apart from the dramatic conflicts so central to this story, the constant shifting of the settings is itself interesting. The reader is seldom left to linger, but is quickly caught up in the action at the next locale, and the trek to Jerusalem stirs up the reader's desire to see just what will happen at the end. The direction of the whole story puts great stress on the ending, the climax in Jerusalem. The settings thus provide an appropriate and integral context for this story. For the settings point toward Jerusalem where the conflicts come to a head and the characters are fully revealed. It is to these conflicts and characters that we now turn.

4

The Plot

We now turn to plot, the events of the story. Some events of a plot form the background or context for the story, while other events constitute the immediate actions in the foreground of the story. The events and actions of a story often involve conflict, for conflict is the heart of most stories. Without conflict, most stories would be only a sequence of events strung together without tension or suspense or struggle on the part of the characters. Although there are many possible approaches to plot, we find the analysis of the conflicts to be helpful as a way to study Mark's plot.[1]

Stories present several kinds of conflict. A character may be in conflict with herself or himself in making a decision, such as Quentin Compson in *The Sound and the Fury;* in conflict with supernatural forces, as Young Goodman Brown is in Hawthorne's story by that name; in conflict with nature, as the old man in Hemingway's *The Old Man and the Sea;* in conflict with other individuals, as are the characters in Bernard Malamud's *The Assistant;* or in conflict with society, as the protagonist in Ralph Ellison's *The Invisible Man.*

In Mark's gospel, the establishment of God's rule provides the larger background for the story. The actions in the foreground focus on the resulting conflicts of the protagonist. Jesus engages in each kind of conflict cited above. He battles the unclean spirits, overcomes threatening forces of nature, confronts the Jewish and gentile authorities, struggles with the disciples, and agonizes within himself about his death. Our analysis of these conflicts includes questions about who initiates the conflict, what issues are at stake, how the conflict escalates, how it is resolved, and the consequences of the resolution. The conflicts in Mark's story interweave and even overlap at significant points, yet each conflict has its own direction, content, ambiance, and resolution. These conflicts in Mark's gospel evoke dramatically intense, emotional, and often violent words and actions. Meanwhile, the narrator builds suspense by gradually escalating the opposition and by leaving the reader in doubt as to the outcome. Finally, the narrator brings the major conflicts to a dramatic conclusion in Jerusalem.

THE BACKGROUND AND ORIGIN OF THE CONFLICTS: GOD'S RULE

Although Jesus is the immediate cause of the conflicts, the story shows that God is the ultimate origin of many of the actions and events of the story.[2] God initiates the first action in the story through the prophecy from Isaiah, a prophecy which declares God's intention to act anew. Beginning with this opening divine announcement, God is establishing rulership over the world. Thus, God's activity provides the larger framework for the story.

God's role in the story can be gleaned from a variety of elements in the narrative: God's words and actions in the story, citations from the writings, riddles, pronouncements of Jesus, and so on.[3] Based on these passages, God's overall role in the story goes like this: God created the world, established a law for the people in the writings and revealed a plan for the future through the prophets. In the words of the riddle, God established a vineyard (Israel) and leased it out to farmers (the Jewish authorities). God sent slaves (prophets) to reap the fruit from the vineyard but the slaves were all mistreated or killed. The farmers used violence to control the vineyard and to prevent the lord of the vineyard from obtaining a rightful share of the produce. The story implies that human authorities have been ruling for themselves rather than God and that Satan has been the strong man in charge of the house. It is at this point in the story world that the narrative opens, with the lord of the vineyard beginning something new by sending his son to the vineyard.

What is new is the beginning of God's rule over the world. The opening lines declare that God's plan, made known in the writings, is about to be established. The time has come. God has sent John to prepare the way, and God has chosen Jesus of Nazareth to be his son, given him authority by the holy spirit, driven him to the desert to confront Satan, and has sent him to announce God's rule and reap the harvest of the vineyard. As authoritative agent of God, Jesus, by his words and actions, affirms that God's rule challenges every other claim to power.[4] The conflicts that result occur in part because of what God is doing; in part, the conflicts occur, too, because people do not recognize God's rule or submit to it. The result is a power struggle between Jesus and those who resist or oppose him.

In the story world, God establishes his rule in two stages. In Mark's gospel the first stage opens with Jesus proclaiming the nearness of the rule of God. Within the imaginative future of the story world, this stage continues after Jesus' death until the second stage, the final establishment of God's rule in power.

In this first stage, the rule of God is hidden and secret. Only those to whom the mystery of the rule of God has been given perceive that the exorcisms and the healings disclose that God has already begun to rule over the world. Jesus preserves the hiddenness of God's rule by talking in riddles and refusing to give signs on demand. Jesus also keeps his identity a secret throughout the story until he is ready to complete his work by facing the consequences of acknowledging his identity. Yet even when the secret of his identity is revealed to others in the story, the hiddenness of God's rule remains, for the truth of Jesus' claim is still hidden to those who do not have the mystery of the rule of God.[5] Furthermore, Jesus invites followers to live a life whose meaning and greatness are hidden to the world. For it is not apparent to most people in Mark's story world that Jesus and his followers, who are persecuted and put to death, are the agents of God's rule. That world does not see God's rule in one who is "least" and a slave, one who has no worldly power or wealth or status, one who is crucified. In the first stage, God establishes his rule by force over all nonhuman powers, giving agents (Jesus, the disciples, others) authority over all nonhuman powers that cause people to suffer: demons, illnesses, afflictions, and the destructive forces of nature. The agents bring God's rule near by overcoming the suffering caused humans by these nonhuman powers. In this conflict God's agents are clearly victors.

God also wills, in this first stage, to establish his rule over humans, but not by force. God's rule is such that people, including agents of God's rule, are to use power to serve others, not to force or oppress them. So, the agents of God invite people to submit to God's rule with repentance, faith and service to others. The people have the opportunity to choose or reject God's rule before it is finally established in power.

Because God's rule challenges all other claims to authority, a conflict ensues between those who choose to proclaim the good news and those who oppose it. Jesus and those who follow him faithfully are at a definite disadvantage in this conflict with the authorities in the story. God's agents have authority to denounce those leaders who do not submit to God's rule and who oppress others, but they have no power or right to stop those oppressors by force. Otherwise, God's agents would themselves be guilty of lording over others. Yet by denouncing the oppressors, God's agents invite oppression upon themselves and become victims of it. In this conflict, Jesus and his followers appear to be the losers.

God's rule thus demands much of those who choose it, because God wills that Jesus and his followers suffer voluntarily in the course of proclaiming the good news. In the story world, God wills that people not suffer from nonhuman powers. But God does will people to suffer from persecution because such suffering is the result of the followers' commitment in a violent world not to lord over others. Such suffering is also a means to further the proclamation of the good news. The necessity for such suffering causes further conflicts: a conflict develops between Jesus who accepts the suffering and his disciples who want to avoid it, and later Jesus is in conflict within himself because he does not want to die.

About halfway through the story, Jesus begins to tell about the final establishment of the rule of God. From this point on in the narrative the imminence of this second stage of the rule of God casts a shadow over all subsequent events. In the future of the story world, this complete establishment of God's rule is to take place before Jesus' generation passes. At that time the hidden rule of God will be made known. Everyone will behold the son of man coming on clouds to gather the chosen ones. God will openly and finally resolve all conflicts, for God will establish his rule "in power." And the resolution will involve a surprising reversal. Those who were great in the eyes of the world, who by human power lorded over others, will be condemned. By contrast, those who lorded over no one, those who lost their lives for Jesus and the good news, will be the greatest. God's agent to rule will be Jesus, the one with the greatest authority who nevertheless died—as the least and a servant for the good news. In the imaginative future of the story world this reversal will be foreshadowed during the generation between Jesus' death and the end: Jesus will be raised, "the farmers of the vineyard" who killed Jesus will be destroyed, and the temple will be desecrated and pulled down. Then the final establishment of God's rule will begin the new age in which those agents who sacrificed and endured for Jesus and the good news will receive eternal life. Even the people who offered those agents of the good news a cup of water will be rewarded.

In summary, the nearness of God's rule in its first stage brings about conflicts because God's hidden rule calls into question every other claim to power and authority, demanding ultimate allegiance. Jesus is the source of the conflicts: dominating the demons and nature, dealing with those who oppose him, and struggling to teach disciples to follow him. The imminent establishment of the second stage of God's rule in power lends an air of urgency and intensity to these conflicts during the first stage, for at that future point all conflicts will ultimately be resolved. The story world will not last beyond one generation before the end occurs. It is within this larger framework of God's rule that we can now examine the specific conflicts in the foreground of the story.

JESUS VERSUS THE DEMONIAC FORCES AND NATURE

Immediately after Jesus becomes God's son, the spirit drives him out to the desert to encounter and be tested by Satan. The depiction of Jesus enduring the forty days, being with angels, and emerging to proclaim the rule of God, suggests that Jesus is the victor in this direct encounter with Satan, a conclusion supported by Jesus' subsequent authority over unclean spirits. In a sense the resolution occurs at the beginning in the desert. Subsequent exorcisms are a result of that resolution.[6]

This conflict with unclean spirits involves displays of power—dramatic and violent, loud and emotionally wrenching. The demons are quite destructive, but the contest is clearly one-sided. John had prophesied that the one to come would be stronger because he would be armed by the power of the holy spirit. With the spirit of God, Jesus is far more powerful than the demons who recognize him as son of God and are afraid of him. For example, the unclean spirit in Capernaum screams at Jesus, "Did you come to destroy us?" Later, the demoniac possessed by "Legion" (whom no one else could subdue) falls before Jesus and pleads that Jesus not torture him. Jesus rebukes the demons easily, driving them out with commands which they immediately obey.

In the cases of Legion and the demoniac boy, Jesus elicits further information in order to effect the exorcism, but there is even then no question what the outcome will be. These exorcisms and the riddle Jesus tells about the strong man depict Jesus as the "stronger one" who has bound the strong man (Satan, in the desert) and is now plundering (exorcising) his goods (the demons). As agent of God's rule, Jesus has authority to destroy unclean spirits.

By quelling demons Jesus demonstrates that God's rule over the world has begun, has come "near." Other displays of power also attest to that. Jesus commands the wind and the sea, provides bread and fish for hungry people in the desert, and causes a fig tree to wither to the roots. Furthermore, Jesus forgives sin, removes leprosy, heals illnesses, removes afflictions, and restores sight, hearing, and a twisted limb. Jesus also empowers his disciples with authority to exorcise and to heal, and he expects them to exercise authority over nature; by faith, they can move mountains. In the world of the story, these powerful acts make it manifest that God is establishing his rule.

The difficult conflicts, however, lie not with demons, for Jesus has authority from God to destroy them. Nor does Jesus struggle much in conflict with nature, for Jesus has authority over it. The difficult conflicts arise with people, for Jesus has no authority to control them; people choose and nothing can be forced upon them. Jesus cannot heal or even exorcise when that act depends on someone's faith and no faith is present. And he is powerless to make people have faith. If the cripple has faith, he will be healed; if the father of the boy with the mute spirit has faith, the demon will be driven out. But when people at Nazareth do not have faith, Jesus is not able to heal them. Jesus has no authority to "lord over" people; he cannot make someone do what he wants them to do. He can order people to be quiet but cannot make them obey (as he can the demons). He can successfully order a deaf-mute to hear and talk, but he cannot make him keep quiet or stop others from listening to him. Furthermore, he cannot make his disciples understand nor can he constrain the authorities to stop opposing him. He cannot control people who, like the opponents and Peter, may unwittingly choose to cooperate with Satan in opposition to Jesus. Thus, Jesus' conflict with Satan indirectly comes to focus in the conflict with people. Because of the limitations on Jesus' authority in relation to people, his conflicts with people are more difficult and more evenly matched than those waged directly with demoniac forces or with nature.

JESUS VERSUS THE AUTHORITIES

The conflict with the authorities sustains suspense. It is not resolved until the end of the story. On account of his courage and cleverness in debate Jesus proves to be superior. Yet the opposition escalates. And Jesus is vulnerable because, as we have seen, he has no authority to dominate people. The suspense builds as to whether they will destroy Jesus, but also whether they will get him on their own terms or his. It is a conflict between the one who thinks the things of God and those who think the things of men—dramatic and hostile, full of tension and trickery. And the resolution, when it comes, is ironic.

General knowledge about first-century Israel helps to explain some of the political and cultural assumptions implicit in these conflicts in the story world.[7] In the narrative, the opponents are more than religious leaders. They are the political authorities at all levels of local and national government. In the story world, as in first-century Israel, there is no distinction between state and religion. Israel was a religious state. The governmental leaders understood themselves to be ruling by God's authority. The laws of the land were the laws believed to have been given by God to Moses and written in the Torah (now the first five books of the Hebrew Bible). There were legal punishments for disobeying these laws, which included the major ordinances (ten commandments) and many civil and criminal regulations. Authorities held trials in synagogues and in the temple; violators were punished, often severely. At the local level, the legal experts indicted people and brought them to trial. In the capital city of Jerusalem, a council (sanhedrin) headed by the High Priest and comprised of high priests, legal experts, and elders, conducted trials in the temple, the center of political/religious authority for the nation. As guardians of law and order in the society, these authorities were responsible not only for interpreting but also for enforcing the laws. Some groups were the recognized interpreters of other scriptural writings as well.

In addition, the whole nation lay under the aegis of the Roman Empire. In Galilee, King Herod deferred to the Roman Emperor, to whom he was responsible. In Judea and Jerusalem, the High Priest and other Jewish authorities were responsible to the procurator, the emperor's representative in the province of Judea. In the story Pilate holds the position of procurator, and he has a cohort of gentile soldiers under him.

Given these implicit political and religious assumptions, one can see more clearly why in the story world Jesus came into conflict with the authorities. He proclaims that God's "rule" has come near, a rule which calls for a new ordering of authority and power, with a consequent reordering of social relationships. He calls for a radical renewal of Israel at the national as well as the individual level in submission to the rule of God. He himself assumes authority as *the* representative of God's rule or "government." He chooses twelve disciples to share the authority, twelve representing the whole of Israel (comprised historically of twelve tribes). He interprets the laws, interprets the writings, abolishes certain traditions and laws, assumes the right to pardon sins, and briefly occupies the national center, the temple, declaring how it should be run. In all his actions and pronouncements, Jesus harshly criticizes the local and national leaders. Thus, what Jesus says and does directly challenges all the authorities in Israel.

To analyze adequately the conflict between Jesus and the authorities, both sides of the conflict need to be articulated. It is difficult to reconstruct the opponent's side, because the narrator does not engage in neutral characterizations, being favorable to Jesus and unsympathetic with the opponents. Nevertheless, the narrator's depiction of the conflict includes clues that reveal the point of view of the authorities in this story.

Authorities' side of the conflict: defending God's Law. As we have seen in an earlier chapter, the opponents, unlike the reader, do not know who Jesus is. Nor do they know about Jesus' baptism, the voice from heaven, or that his actions fulfill the writings. They do not have access to Jesus' private teaching to the disciples, and they are not present at many of his public actions. We can base our evaluation of the opponents as characters only on what they observe of Jesus or apparently hear about him. The opponents contend that Jesus assumes extensive legal authority for himself, interprets the law in ways they consider illegal, and disregards many religious customs. They respond by trying to get charges against him for his illegal behavior.

The local legal experts are the first opponents to encounter Jesus in the house at Capernaum. They see Jesus daring to pardon sins, a right reserved only for God in Israelite law. (In ancient Israel the High Priest alone entered the inner sanctuary of the temple once a year to ask God for pardon of national sins.) Yet in Capernaum this charismatic Galilean claims that *he* has the authority to pardon sins, to do what only God does through the temple system. The opponents react (inwardly) in shock at Jesus' audacity; they immediately identify his words as blasphemy against God, a charge punishable by death![8]

Similarly, the authorities are taken aback by Jesus' actions on the Sabbath. They treat offenses against the Sabbath law as serious illegalities. Assumed in the story is the notion that according to "the writings," the Sabbath rest was built into the act of creation itself (the seventh day) and the Sabbath law was one of the ten "commandments." In the culture of Israel it was forbidden to work on the Sabbath in order to guarantee time for worship and rest. Furthermore, the Sabbath was a cornerstone of Jewish society. In the ancient world, certain traditions and customs unified the Jews and distinguished them from other nationalities. The Sabbath was perhaps the most obvious of these observances; to disregard it threatened Jewish identity and the fabric of their society. The same assumptions are operative in the story where the authorities take the Sabbath laws very seriously. When the disciples pick grain on the Sabbath, the authorities accuse them of doing "what is not legal"; and they hold Jesus responsible by asking him about their behavior. In his answer Jesus claims that the son of man (that is, Jesus) is lord over the Sabbath, with the right to interpret Sabbath laws. In response to such an extreme claim, the Pharisees begin to watch to see whether Jesus will heal on the Sabbath so they can bring charges against him, charges which, like blasphemy, could carry the death penalty.[9] The seriousness of the Sabbath offense is underscored when the Pharisees, unable here to secure evidence against Jesus, go off to hold a council with the Herodians to plan to destroy him.

Thus, early in the story Jesus assumes for himself rights and prerogatives traditionally associated with two central institutions of Israel: the temple and the official legal interpreters. Jesus' actions are so opposed to what the authorities accept as God's laws that they conclude Jesus could not be acting on God's authority. As a result, they assume that

Jesus' healings and exorcisms did not come from God; the exorcism of someone so blasphemous could only come by authority of Satan. Legal experts, therefore, come from Jerusalem to discredit him by labeling him as possessed.

The authorities are also disturbed at Jesus' disregard for the oral "traditions of the elders," the most important of which relate to the avoidance of contact with that which is unclean. In the story all Jews, and especially Pharisees, cleanse their hands before eating. By implication, they believed that only those who belonged to the covenant of God's chosen people were holy. To keep holy to God and to avoid contamination from pagan influence, Jews avoided contact with gentiles. Since that was next to impossible, especially at the markets, they performed a symbolic rite of cleansing by washing their hands up to the elbow before eating. Also, they cleansed food and utensils. These rituals were important because they preserved the uniqueness of Jewish culture and kept the Jews holy to God. In the story, Jesus and his disciples observed none of these traditions from the elders. When the authorities see the disciples eating with "defiled" hands and Jesus dining with toll collectors and sinners (unclean from their regular contact with gentiles),[10] they ask Jesus to explain these actions.

The authorities are also exasperated by what they perceive to be Jesus' trickery in debate, for he uses his knowledge of the law to defeat them. He even tells them they do not know the writings, several times asking them, "Haven't you ever read . . . ?" Jesus' cleverness in debate undermines their authority with the crowds, especially evident in the series of encounters between Jesus and the authorities in Jerusalem. When the authorities try to pin Jesus down, he is evasive and often cryptic. He tells riddles against them, and they do not understand what the riddles mean. They flatter him in order to get an incriminating answer in Jerusalem, but the irony of their flattery reveals the authorities' thoughts: they are convinced Jesus is *not* truthful and that he looks for the "reactions of men"; otherwise, he would give them straight answers. The authorities' response to Jesus' verbal maneuvers is a greater determination to bring charges against Jesus for his actions.

Jesus' challenge to the authorities comes to a climax with his attack on the temple which the authorities consider most threatening and offensive. The buying and selling in the temple were meant to preserve the holiness of the temple; unblemished doves were sold for sacrificing, and pagan coins were exchanged for sacred temple money. Jesus violently upends the tables and chairs used for these purposes, driving the people out, prohibiting traffic through the temple area, and citing the writings in defense of his action. The high priests see his action as an attack upon them and the temple. They also see Jesus' action as a threat to law and order. They fear that popular support for Jesus will lead to a riot, so they are afraid to arrest Jesus during the festival. By his action in the temple, Jesus is undermining national authority. In response, the authorities decide to get rid of him, arrest him at night, and marshal the evidence at the trial. At Jesus' trial, the authorities seek evidence to convict Jesus of blasphemous pronouncements against the temple, and some witnesses even testify that Jesus made prophetic statements about pulling down the temple.

But the narrator resolves the legal conflicts between Jesus and the authorities on other grounds. The probing questions of the High Priest during the trial result in Jesus' confession. Jesus finally admits openly and plainly who he claims to be: he acknowledges the High Priest's incriminating suggestion that he is the anointed one, the son of the Blessed One, and he does so by using the highly provocative phrase "I am," a claim to divine prerogatives; he also cryptically claims that he (as son of man) will sit on the right hand of God; and he implies that the authorities will be judged when they behold God as "the Powerful One." This cluster of statements—particularly the human claim of divine prerogatives—gives the Sanhedrin the evidence they need. The statement is legally intolerable; they convict him of blasphemy and sentence him to death.[11] Their subsequent mockery of Jesus shows how they consider Jesus' claims for himself to be inordinate and ridiculous.

Jesus' side of the conflict: message and evasion. Jesus has been anointed to usher in God's rule. The issue for Jesus is how to get the authorities to "see" God's authority in his actions and teaching. Throughout the confrontations with authorities, Jesus does, in one way or another, explain his views. In debate, Jesus often addresses the authorities with a rhetorical question (or two) followed by a teaching (or action) which answers the rhetorical question he has posed. That Jesus answers the questions he himself raises shows that he wants to get across a message, at least to those who have ears to hear. Nevertheless, when their minds harden against him, he speaks to them in riddles.

Jesus must deal with the authorities, once they have turned against him. Much of what he says and does in the course of proclaiming the rule of God is open to criminal charges; therein lies the difficulty. For example, Jesus does not explicitly make public claims that he is the anointed one or the son of God; he commands the demons (who call him the son of God) to shut up; and when the disciples identify him as the anointed one, he tells them to keep quiet. At his trial we discover why Jesus hides his identity. Upon openly declaring who he is, the authorities condemn him to death for blasphemy. The dilemma for Jesus is this: how can he inaugurate God's rule, yet evade the efforts of the authorities to trap him? Many aspects of the secrecy motif are related to this problem.

The dilemma is complicated by Jesus' limitations. He has no power from God to force the opponents to accept him, and in faithfulness to the rule of God he does not try to dominate them by ordinary means. So he must use his wits to convey his message and at the same time avoid indictment. This he does by several means: clever methods of healing, cryptic statements, riddles, and his superior knowledge of the laws and of the other writings.

Jesus sometimes heals cleverly to evade indictment. For example, when Jesus pardons the cripple, legal experts consider it blasphemy. Jesus knows that if he repeats himself he will be open to indictment. Instead, he heals the man and thereby evades indictment, since healing is not blasphemy! At the same time, he conveys his message by explaining that healing is the same as a pardon (since removal of the consequences of sin implies a pardon of sin). He even tells the legal experts that they should see from the healing that he has authority to pardon sins. In a similar instance, when Pharisees watch to see if he will heal on the Sabbath, Jesus cleverly heals a man simply by telling him to stretch out his hand. Jesus never touches him nor does he directly speak a word of healing; so technically he is not legally liable for work on the Sabbath! In both instances Jesus expresses his authority and explains his action, yet foils the authorities' efforts to indict him.[12]

Jesus also avoids incriminating himself by means of cryptic self-references, such as "the son of man." If he had said to the legal experts "*I* have authority on earth to pardon sins," he would have exposed himself again to a charge of blasphemy. But he refers to himself in the third person as "the son of man," a phrase ambiguous enough to refer

to someone else or to all humanity. The same can be said of his statement, "The son of man is lord even of the Sabbath." By so speaking
Jesus claims a superiority over the Sabbath—the unique right to interpret the Sabbath laws and by implication the law as a whole. But
because this claim follows a general proverbial saying about the
Sabbath having been originated for "man," the referent "the son of
man" is too uncertain to be used as evidence against Jesus. The epithet
"son of man" serves a variety of functions throughout the story, but in
these episodes it enables Jesus to affirm his authority without incriminating himself.

Jesus occasionally avoids indictment by talking in riddles. For
example, when the authorities accuse Jesus of exorcising by authority
of Satan, Jesus recounts an allegorical riddle in which he affirms that he
has bound Satan and is plundering his goods (exorcising). In a
cryptic saying which follows, he adds that his authority is really the holy
spirit. In the context of the story—given Jesus' other actions—these
claims, spoken plainly, would have invited a charge of blasphemy.
Later, Jesus talks in a riddle to obscure his pronouncement that all
foods are to be considered clean, an action which would have been
open to the charge of nullifying and superseding sacred written laws.
But the meaning of the riddle escaped the authorities from Jerusalem,
and Jesus explains it only in private to the disciples.

In Jerusalem Jesus again uses riddles to avoid an explicit answer to
the opponents' question, "By what authority are you doing these
things?" Through the allegorical elements of a riddle about a vineyard,
Jesus answers their question cryptically, explaining that he is God's son,
that he has authority from God, and that the opponents will be
destroyed for their opposition. The authorities know he has aimed the
riddle at them, but are frustrated in their attempts to get direct
evidence against him. Through some of the riddles Jesus avoids incrimi-
nation, yet conveys his message for those who "have ears to hear."

Also, Jesus uses his superior knowledge of the legal and prophetic
writings to justify his actions and to defend against criminal accusations. For example, he cites the passage about David eating bread in
the temple as a precedent for his disciples' picking grain on the
Sabbath. Sometimes he responds to an accusing question based on one
law by citing another law he considers to be more important; for
example, God's original purpose for marriage takes precedence over

Moses' permission to divorce, and laws requiring love take precedence over laws requiring sacrifices. Several times Jesus cleverly turns a trick question back on the opponents in order to reveal a weakness in their opinions or the hypocrisy of their questions. He does this in his responses to the question about the source of his authority and to the question about taxes. Jesus also quotes the writings to explain his attack on the temple. These techniques in debate serve on the one hand to give a legal basis for his actions and on the other hand to keep the opponents from catching him in his words. About matters of "tradition," Jesus has the freedom to act and talk openly since in the story there are no legal penalties for breaking traditions.

The development of the conflict in the plot. The narrator has carefully structured Jesus' conflict with the opponents so as to create tension and suspense. In the five initial clashes between Jesus and the authorities in Galilee this is clear. The opposition against Jesus widens. The groups opposing Jesus expand in number. One by one, each new group is introduced into an association with a previously introduced group of opponents: first the local legal experts, then the legal experts of the Pharisees, then the Pharisees, then the Pharisees with the Herodians. Similarly, the narrator creates suspense by gradually intensifying the opponents' efforts to get Jesus: first the opponents accuse Jesus in thought only; then they question the disciples about Jesus' actions; next they query Jesus directly about an offense against a custom; after that, they ask Jesus about the illegal behavior of the disciples; then they watch Jesus in order to get charges against him; and finally they go off and plot to destroy him. As opposition propels the action forward, Jesus' responses intensify. At first, he tries appealing to the authorities by action and explanation, but he soon becomes angry and saddened by the hardening of their minds. By the end of the five conflict episodes the sides are clearly established.[13]

During the remainder of Jesus' activity in Galilee the sides become firmly established. The opposition expands to include legal experts from Jerusalem, Herod, and then Pharisees from Jerusalem. The verbal exchanges intensify when the authorities from Jerusalem slander him by intimating that he is possessed. Later the authorities try to discredit him by accusing him of not following the tradition of the elders and by asking him to give a sign of his authority. Meanwhile

Jesus pronounces an interdict against their unpardonable sin, and when it becomes clear to him that they are "on the outside," he tells riddles to obscure his message further. Also, after calling the Pharisees hypocrites, he proclaims a prophecy against them.

The impending clash with authorities dominates the journey to Jerusalem even though the presence of the authorities hardly figures in these episodes. In prophesying his death Jesus identifies the legal experts, the elders, the high priests, and the gentiles as the ones who will reject him and kill him in Jerusalem. Only once on the journey do the authorities figure in the action. When Jesus returns to John's former territory around the Jordan, the Pharisees try to maneuver him into making the same statement about marriage and divorce which resulted in John's death by Herod. But by now the threat from opponents in Galilee has begun to fade as Jesus enters the capital city.

The climactic confrontation in Jerusalem comes quickly. Jesus attacks and briefly occupies the temple, the national center of government. The opponents again state their determination to destroy Jesus, with all the national authorities fully marshaled against Jesus. Again, opposition escalates: first, the authorities want to destroy him; after that they seek a way to seize him; then they seek a way to seize him by a deception. This plan is completed when Judas appears; and finally they do seize him. Meanwhile, Jesus prevails in the debates with authorities, prophesies their destruction, and launches scathing attacks against some of the legal experts. Although verbal and reasoned opposition to Jesus dissipates, the authorities decide to arrest him anyway and establish the evidence at the trial.[14] There the climax of the conflict comes when Jesus makes a final pronouncement against them and they sentence him to death. After that, the conflict subsides: his sentence is carried out by the gentile authorities; the Jewish leaders ridicule him; and Jesus is silent.

It is noteworthy in the plotting of the conflict that the first accusation against Jesus—which is articulated in the mind only—is the charge of blasphemy, the very charge upon which the authorities finally condemn him to death.[15] So from the very beginning of the story Jesus walks a tightrope—under constant threat—and must evade incriminating charges until the right time. His narrow escape from such a serious charge early in the story contributes significantly to the tension and suspense in this conflict.

Consequently, throughout, the reader wonders just how Jesus will deal with the widening and intensifying opposition against him. Nevertheless, the reader sees that Jesus is firmly in control. He regularly evades indictment, wins in debates, and, except at his trial, he always has the last word. The authorities are unable to obtain evidence against Jesus unless he gives it to them. At the trial, Jesus himself volunteers the evidence they need. He thus controls when his opponents will win the indictment, as well as the specific charge they level against him. Only the claim of who he is, which they judge to be blasphemy, provides the grounds for his conviction. Jesus, not the authorities, determines his fate.[16]

The resolution of the conflict. The narrator resolves the conflict between Jesus and the authorities only when the authorities condemn Jesus and put him to death. It is an ironic resolution.[17] The authorities think they have eliminated Jesus, proved him not to be the anointed one, and ended the messianic matter. But the opposite situation prevails. In actuality, they have cooperated in bringing about God's plan. Jesus wants the same resolution they have sought and helps to bring it about, though for very different reasons. He has done so in obedience to God, who wills that Jesus give his life for many. Jesus knows that it is ultimately God, not the authorities, who will "strike the shepherd."

Furthermore, through the ironic resolution, the story depicts Jesus as the real authority in Israel. The hidden truth of the sarcastic accusations leveled against Jesus establishes him as the true king of Israel. By contrast, the story reveals the opponents to be false authorities. By their involvement in Jesus' death, they reveal themselves to be envious, destructive, and blind to the way in which God rules in the world. It is *they* who have been on trial and are here condemned. They condemn as blasphemy Jesus' claim to be son of God, but since, in the story world, Jesus' claim is true, *they* are the ones guilty of blasphemy.[18] By condemning and executing God's son, they have rejected God, been guilty of the eternal sin, and sealed their own doom.

This irony is of course hidden from the authorities, but it is not hidden from the reader. And the discerning reader can see that the apparent resolution will be reversed in the final establishment of God's rule, prophesied by Jesus. The reader sees that reversal initiated in the episode of the empty tomb. The final reversal will occur in the imminent future of the story world, within a generation, when the ironic resolution will be fully unveiled: Jesus will be established in power and the authorities condemned. Jesus foreshadows this ultimate reversal when, at his trial, he says that the son of man will come on the right hand of God and that the authorities will behold God as the "Powerful One." Jesus predicts, therefore, that this ultimate reversal will occur in the imminent future of the story world. But the reader encounters the ironic resolution, the hidden resolution, as the last word in the plotted narrative.

JESUS AND THE DISCIPLES

Jesus initiates the circumstances of conflict with the disciples by calling them to follow him and by expecting so much of them: to be fishers for men, to understand him, and to have faith to move mountains. Later, he introduces even higher standards for discipleship: to renounce the self, lose one's life, be the least, and be a servant or slave to others. At stake in this conflict is whether Jesus can make them good disciples. The disciples sacrifice much to follow Jesus and they show great determination to remain loyal to him. They are fascinated and awed by Jesus, yet he leads them toward that which they do not want to face. From their point of view, his expectations and demands are just too much for them. The disciples struggle at every point to follow Jesus but are simply overwhelmed by both him and his demands.

In this conflict, Jesus is not so superior. His task is difficult. His efforts to lead the disciples to understand are more than equaled by their hardness of mind and their fear. The clash between the things of God and the things of men is similar to Jesus' clash with the authorities. Yet the challenge is different. The conflict with the authorities concerns people in determined opposition to Jesus. The clash with disciples concerns those who are trying to be his followers.[19] The suspense lies in his best, almost desperate, efforts at teaching, correcting, demonstrating, and warning; whether Jesus will succeed in making them good disciples is in constant question. This uncertainty remains intact in the indeterminacy of resolution.

The disciples' side of the conflict: too much too fast. From the start, the disciples do not know much about Jesus. They do not know about his baptism, the voice from heaven, or about his confrontation with Satan in the desert. And Jesus does not tell them who he is. Yet when he calls them, they leave everything and follow him wherever he goes. Later, when he summons them to the mountain so he might appoint the twelve, they go off to meet him. They succeed in becoming fishers for men: they proclaim and have authority to drive out demons and heal. And they have no conflicts with Jesus on matters of law and tradition, as the authorities do.

However, when Jesus begins to talk in riddles, they do not understand. When they first ask Jesus about a riddle, they are told that they have been given the mystery of the rule of God and are supposed to understand. And they are reprimanded for *not* understanding. Later, when they ask him about a riddle concerning defilement, they are chastised again; they are expected to understand a riddle which even the legal experts did not understand.

The disciples are also expected to understand the awesome acts of Jesus and to perform the same acts themselves. For example, they react with understandable fright and fear to the storm and with even more to Jesus' power over the wind and sea. Yet Jesus reprimands them for being cowards and not having faith. They become so overwhelmed that they cannot be aware that Jesus expects them to have taken charge of the storm themselves. Similarly, they are terrified when Jesus walks toward them on the sea. On other occasions, they are mystified when Jesus expects them to be able to feed huge crowds in the desert. And they remain at a loss as to what Jesus' acts of power mean about his identity.

The disciples are not told explicitly and clearly what these acts mean or how they are expected to repeat them. To the disciples, Jesus' actions and expectations occur without preparation or direction. The disciples' spoken responses to Jesus, framed mostly in single rhetorical questions, reveal their incredulity: "So who is this that even the wind and the sea obey him?" "You're looking at the crowd pressing against you, and you say 'who touched me?'?" "Surely we're not to go off and buy two hundred denarii worth of bread and give it to them to eat?" "How will anyone be able to feed all these people here in a desert?"

The conflict reaches a climax when the disciples completely miss the point of Jesus' teaching about the "leaven" of the Pharisees, who require signs to have faith. Suddenly, the disciples have a spate of rhetorical questions hurled at them, the assertion of which is that they are deaf and blind, and that their minds are hardened. They are expected to understand something about the rule of God but have never been told in a straightforward way what it is. Jesus' statements and actions have been so mystifying that they do not know what it is they are to understand. Finally, Peter identifies Jesus as the anointed one. In response, however, Jesus urges them to keep quiet about his identity, and then he confronts the disciples with the most surprising development of all. He tells the disciples that he will be rejected by the authorities and put to death. Peter cannot accept Jesus' statement, for the idea is intolerable to him. Jesus then turns on him, calling him Satan and telling him that he is not thinking the things of God. Jesus then establishes an entirely new standard for discipleship: whoever wants to follow him should renounce the self and take up a cross. The disciples have come this far with Jesus, only to be told that the anointed one will be put to death and that they too will die by persecution at the end of the way.

On their journey to Jerusalem, a series of clashes takes place between Jesus and the disciples—clashes which reflect the difference between what the disciples expect from following Jesus and what Jesus expects of them. The disciples share the expectations of the leaders in the world of the story, who assume that when the anointed one comes, God will establish him in Israel with power and glory. The disciples consider that if Jesus is the anointed one they can only benefit from their association with him. The disciples expect that by following Jesus they will save their lives. Having left everything for the rule of God and now being among Jesus' inner twelve, they expect eventual prosperity (to gain the world), importance, and positions of power as Jesus establishes God's rule in Israel. What they had previously experienced of Jesus in the story until now reinforced these expectations: the healings, exorcisms, works of power over nature, and the huge crowds. And they had been told only that they would be fishers for men. There have been few if any clues so far to suggest that Jesus' mission would be other than what they expected. Now, however, Jesus tells them three times that he will be rejected and killed, and that they too must renounce themselves and lose their lives.

At a deeper level, this conflict between Jesus and the disciples on the way to Jerusalem exemplifies the clash between the values of the disciples and those of Jesus. The disciples share the values of the authorities. The disciples hope to prosper, to be important and powerful. They are shocked that a godly, wealthy man will not receive eternal life. Having assumed that wealth is to be sought as a sign of God's favor, they ask incredulously, "So who is able to be saved?" But Jesus defines their values as "thinking the things of men" and turns those values upside down with paradoxical statements: losing their lives to save them, being least or like children to be first, being a slave or a servant to be great. The disciples are expected to surrender the basic expectations they have had about life and about God. They are overwhelmed and confused by these new teachings, and only gradually are they able to accept them.[20]

Furthermore, the disciples have received few words of praise. They are reprimanded, corrected, or warned about almost everything they do. By the end of the journey to Jerusalem, Jesus has promised them nothing for their sacrifices. Only now, when Peter reminds Jesus how they left everything to follow him, are they told of a reward. In this age, they are to receive a hundred times as many family members and as much property as they left behind (referring to the many families and houses they visit on their travels from village to village) but "with persecutions!" In the coming age (the final stage of the rule of God), they are to receive eternal life; but, Jesus adds threateningly, "many who are most important [the disciples?] will be least, and the least most important."

Despite all that happens on the journey, the loyal disciples follow Jesus to Jerusalem. Then, after this extensive preparation for his death and theirs, Jesus tells them that none will be faithful: one will hand him over; all will stumble and be scattered; and Peter will renounce him. They are incredulous and refuse to accept these predictions. Throughout the story, Jesus has had the final say in each conflict with disciples; but in this clash, the disciples have the final word. Peter says, "Even if I have to die with you, I'll definitely not renounce you." Through this change in the pattern of who has the final word, the story emphasizes the disciples' determination to die with Jesus.[21]

However, events move too quickly. Jesus has not warned the disciples that they will fail until the threatening events are imminent. That very night they are to keep watch yet they are unprepared and fall asleep. The crowd comes to arrest him—unexpectedly in the night— and acting on the impulse of fear they flee. Peter follows Jesus but is discovered in the courtyard. He too abandons Jesus. These final circumstances of the disciples seem to typify their whole struggle to be faithful followers of Jesus. They simply are not prepared for the unpredictable, overwhelming consequences of following Jesus. Everything overwhelms them; everything happens too quickly. The final depiction of Peter, sobbing after his third denial of Jesus, is a stark portrayal of how much the disciples want to succeed and how utterly, at the end of the gospel, they fail.

Jesus' side of the conflict: frustration. Jesus chooses disciples, but he simply cannot lead them to understand him or do what he expects of them. He calls the disciples to join with him in proclaiming the rule of God and in bringing it near—by exorcisms and healings. He does not reveal his identity, for he does not tell anyone who he is. All characters are left to "see" for themselves who Jesus is.

Jesus assumes that the disciples will understand him and the rule of God, for they have left everything and followed him. When they do not understand the riddles about the rule of God, his response indicates that he is shocked and surprised. Although he unravels the riddles privately for the disciples, their subsequent behavior suggests they still do not understand. Jesus also assumes that they will know who he is by his actions, yet he only frightens and disorients them further. They seem unable to understand the most dramatic works of power or the most direct warnings. In his impatience and frustration, Jesus hurls rhetorical questions at them so that they may see how blind and dense they are. The result is silence.

Based on their initial response to him, Jesus assumes that the disciples will have faith, and he gives them opportunities to show it. Jesus expects them to have faith during the storm at sea. When they do not, he is surprised and calms the storm himself. But they learn nothing from his action, for when he later gives them a chance to deal with the wind and sea on their own, they only struggle at the oars. Jesus expects them to have faith to feed a crowd in the desert. When they do not understand that expectation, Jesus shows them by having them distribute the food. Later, he gives them another chance to supply food for a crowd in the desert, but they are incredulous, as if they had not even witnessed the first feeding.[22] When, after these two feedings, the disciples for a third time are still worried, this time about having only one loaf of bread in the boat, Jesus becomes especially impatient and asks them a series of leading questions. Still they do not understand.[23] Later in Jerusalem, this same conflict over what is possible by faith continues: Peter expresses surprise that the fig tree withered. In this last episode, Jesus finally tells them openly about the power of faith rather than simply demonstrating it.

Jesus becomes especially upset when he realizes that his own disciples are blind like the authorities. He reprimands them severely when they do not understand the riddle about defilement any better than the authorities do. After giving two signs in the desert and warning them about the leaven of the Pharisees and Herod, he is shocked to discover that, like the authorities', the disciples' minds are hardened. On the journey to Jerusalem, when the disciples mirror the oppressive behavior of the authorities, Jesus is most dramatic in his efforts to change them: he "rebukes" Peter, calling him Satan; he warns the disciples to cut off limbs if necessary; he gets angry; he alerts them to the imminent establishment of the rule of God in power; he warns them that they might not enter the rule of God and that in the new age they might be least.

These conflicts are intensified by Jesus' urgent need to prepare the disciples for his impending death. For when Peter finally sees that Jesus is the anointed one, Jesus' task shifts. Not only must he lead them to accept the idea that as the anointed one he will be rejected and put to death, he must also convince them that it is God's will; it is a "necessary" part of God's plan for him to die this way. Otherwise they will not even see the meaning of his death. Three times Jesus predicts his death and each time he must deal with their resistance and denseness.

Also, Jesus clearly states the reality that if they are to follow him, they too must be ready to die. Jesus warns them not to seek suffering in order to gain rewards of power or status. The focus of their behavior should be on service for others and proclaiming the good news, which they are to embrace simply because it is what God's rule requires of people. But Jesus must prepare them for death, because they are sure to encounter suffering in the course of living for him and the good news. If they are not prepared to die, they will not be able to follow. Thus, Jesus experiences frustration and anger on the journey, because the attitudes and behavior of the disciples run contrary to what he teaches them about his death, their death, and the values of the rule of God.

Moreover, Jesus urgently tries to prepare the disciples for his absence.[24] He says early on that, like John's disciples, they will be left on their own. Much later, when his disciples do not even yet have enough faith to exorcise a powerful demon, Jesus says in exasperation, "O faithless generation! How long am I to be with you? How long am I to put up with you?" On the way to Jerusalem, he is direct and harsh. He gives them no false assurances. He is trying to prepare them for the worst after his death. Then, in Jerusalem, he prepares them further by foretelling what conflicts and persecutions will happen after his death. He does not know how the disciples will cope with these events, but he announces his impending absence, warns them not to be led astray, and admonishes them to keep watch for his return.

Yet Jesus knows that, despite preparing them for his death and their death, they will fail in Jerusalem. He anticipates this failure by telling them that they will all stumble and by promising to go ahead of them to Galilee after he is raised. In spite of their protests to the contrary, Jesus knows they will flee and deny him. Yet even Jesus is surprised at the extent of their failure: they fall asleep and do not even support him by keeping watch.[25] His last words to them express a frantic effort to arouse them from sleep in order to support him in the face of arrest.

The development of the conflict in the plot. Because the conflict is harsh and frustrating between these two aligned parties, it causes great tension for the reader. And since the reader aligns with Jesus, the reader has an interest in seeing how the disciples will fare. Since Jesus makes great efforts on behalf of the disciples, the reader wants them to succeed. The conflict involves suspense.

This suspense rises and falls with the conflict reaching a climax in Jerusalem.[26] In Galilee, the conflict centers around Jesus' acts of power and his riddles. The clash over the disciples' lack of faith to do acts of power other than healings and exorcisms continues throughout the story. But their inability to understand Jesus comes to a climax in the third boat scene, and is partially resolved when Peter subsequently identifies Jesus as the anointed one. This resolution, however, leads to further conflict, not about Jesus' identity, but about the notion that he will be rejected and die, and that the same fate is expected for the disciples. This conflict is resolved when the disciples show their determination to die with Jesus. Finally, this resolution in turn leads to the final conflict with death itself.

The conflict between the disciples and Jesus over his expectations of them reflects in part a conflict within the disciples. They want to be loyal to Jesus, but they also do not want to give up everything, especially their lives. When all other considerations are stripped away, the conflict comes down to a struggle within the disciples themselves between loyalty and survival. They want to be loyal, but when loyalty takes them face to face with death, their instincts for survival are too strong.

Resolution. The resolution to the conflict is negative. Although the disciples become fishers for men, understand that Jesus is the anointed one, and accept both Jesus' death and the notion that they are to die with Jesus, nevertheless they are not prepared to lose their lives. They fail at renouncing self and taking up a cross. Jesus does not succeed in making them faithful disciples.

The questions remain: In the imaginative future of the story world, what will be the result of this resolution? Will there be a new resolution? Will the disciples learn from failure and follow Jesus faithfully after his death? Will the conflict be resolved favorably in the future of the story world? Jesus does not disown the disciples for their behavior. Jesus' loyalty to them lasts beyond his death into the future of the story world, for he makes a covenant with the disciples at the Passover meal and then promises to go ahead of them to Galilee. Nevertheless, after Jesus' resurrection the disciples will be without Jesus until his return in power and glory; from the time of his resurrection Jesus will be absent from the world at the right hand of God. He will be like the master of the house away on a trip, while the disciples are waiting for his return. The reader wonders how the disciples will fare in Jesus' absence if they have already fared so poorly when he is present. In any case, Jesus has done all he can do for them; any new resolution to the conflict will depend not on Jesus but on the disciples themselves. The narrator leaves this fate of the disciples in the future of the story world undetermined.[27]

The Plot

This indeterminacy or lack of an ultimate resolution reveals itself when we look at the ambiguity of the ending. The young man at the tomb says to the woman: "Go tell his disciples, even Peter, 'He's going ahead of you to Galilee. There you will behold him just as he told you.'" Everything about this statement suggests the possibility of restoration. Simon is again called Peter, his discipleship name (Jesus addressed him as Simon at Gethsemane!). Jesus is still "going ahead" of them and they are to follow. Furthermore, the instruction to go to Galilee points to the possibility of a new start, a movement from rejection in Jerusalem toward proclaiming the good news to gentiles. There is, therefore, a pointer at the end suggesting that the disciples will go back to Galilee and there behold Jesus.

But this is not the end of the story. The women at the tomb flee in fear and say nothing to anyone at all, including the disciples. The message to the disciples through the women is aborted yet the reader recalls that Jesus himself had earlier said that he would go ahead of them to Galilee. However, at the time Jesus said this, the disciples totally ignored him because they were preoccupied with resisting Jesus' prophecy that they would stumble. Given the depiction of the disciples throughout the story, the reader is led to think that Jesus' statement made no impression on them. The end of the story leads the reader to conclude that the disciples will not go to Galilee, will not therefore see Jesus or be restored. So the reader remains uncertain.

The indeterminate resolution leads the reader to review the story for clues about the fate of the disciples in the future of the story world. These clues include the prophecies Jesus makes about the disciples, the conditional warnings he addresses to them, and the admonitions.

The prophecies about the disciples which come to fulfillment within the narrative lead the reader to assume that other prophecies Jesus makes about the disciples will be fulfilled later in the future of the story world. Jesus prophesies to James and John that they will drink the cup he drinks and be baptized by the baptism with which he is to be baptized (die by persecution). He tells the disciples that they will receive a hundred times more in families and possessions from the hospitality they will experience in their travels from town to town—with persecutions. He tells four disciples on the Mountain of the Olives that they will be beaten in synagogues, handed over to Sanhedrins, stand before governors and kings as testimony to him, and be hated by

97

everyone because of his name. Elsewhere Jesus states in a similar vein that everyone will be salted with fire. Also, Jesus suggests that the disciples will recount the event of his transformation on the mountain after his resurrection and that the good news will be proclaimed in the whole world. All these prophecies affirm that the disciples will continue to follow Jesus and will suffer in the course of proclaiming his good news of the rule of God. Although it is not clear that the disciples go to Galilee to behold Jesus, nevertheless, these prophecies suggest some kind of restoration and continuing discipleship.

What prophecies are made by Jesus about the ultimate fate of the disciples when the rule of God is established in power? Throughout the story, Jesus gives the disciples almost no assurance of their ultimate fate. He says he will drink wine anew in the rule of God, but he does not tell the disciples that they will be present. Only once does Jesus assure the disciples by affirming that there is no one who has left family and possessions for him and the good news who will not receive the eternal life in the age to come. Yet he adds that those who are most important now will be least then. There will be gradations of reward and position in the eternal life of the coming age. James and John will not sit on Jesus' right and left. And because all the disciples are preoccupied with greatness, they may perhaps be least.

This uncertainty about the disciples' fate is reinforced by other conditional warnings which suggest that the fate of the disciples in the rule of God could be jeopardized by their behavior: "Whoever wants to save his life will lose it"; "Whoever is ashamed of me and my words . . . , also the son of man will be ashamed of him"; "Whoever causes one of these little ones who have faith to stumble, it would be better . . ."; "Whoever does not receive the rule of God like a little child will definitely not enter it"; "Whoever endures to the end will be saved." Within the plotted narrative, the disciples fail to heed every one of these warnings and, therefore, come under the threat of the interdicts attached to the conditions.

Although the disciples failed to heed these warnings, there is the offer of forgiveness. Early on, Jesus says that all sins would be pardoned the sons of men except the sin against the holy spirit. In Jerusalem, Jesus tells the disciples that if they pardon the offenses of others, the Father in heaven will pardon their offenses. Jesus' continued commitment to the disciples implies that they are pardoned and restored for their failures. Yet the possibility also exists that, in the future of the story world, they may again fail to heed the warnings and again come under the interdicts: they may be ashamed of Jesus, cause someone to stumble, or not endure to the end. Given how consistently the disciples fail in the plotted story and how slowly they learn, the reader wonders whether they will behave any differently in the future.

This lack of resolution in Jesus' conflict with the disciples is further reinforced by the warnings Jesus gives to the disciples. He warns them not to cause stumbling, to let no false prophet or anointed one mislead them, not to be alarmed at wars or report about wars, to preach the good news to all the gentile nations, not to be anxious when brought to trial but to say what the spirit gives them to say, to flee Judea when they see the desolating horror in the sanctuary, and to look out, keep watch, and stay awake or the son of man might return unexpectedly in the "evening" or at "midnight" or at the "rooster crow" or "early in the morning," and find them sleeping.

We are not told whether the disciples will heed any of these warnings in the future of the story world. We do know, however, that Peter, James, and John ignored some of these warnings at Gethsemane. They failed to "keep watch." Three times Jesus found them sleeping. The disciples also failed in the "evening" when Judas went off to hand him over, in the "middle of the night" when they fled, at the "rooster crow" when Peter renounced him,[28] and "early in the morning" when no disciple was left to witness his ordeal. Such failures suggest that these and the other warnings might also not be heeded in the future.

If the narrator had ended the story with the glorious reunion, the reader would assume that the disciples' fate in the rule of God was favorably assured. But the narrator does not end the story this way. And given the repeated failures of the disciples, the lack of assurance from Jesus, and the aborted message at the end, the reader can only conclude that the narrator has deliberately left the future of the disciples uncertain. Their ultimate fate in the rule of God is conditional upon their behavior in the period from the death of Jesus to the return of the son of man. However, the narrator does make it clear that soon all will come to light. In the imaginative future of the story world, the son of man will return within their generation, at which time the fate of the disciples in the rule of God is to be decided. That is, all conflicts in the story will be resolved ultimately when the rule of God is established in power and the new age inaugurated.

Summary. We have dealt separately with the conflict between Jesus and the authorities and the conflict between Jesus and the disciples. As we noted earlier, these conflicts are somewhat isolated from each other in the story world by means of the public and private settings. Also, except at the end, the disciples never come directly into conflict with the authorities, although such a clash is prophesied to occur in the future of the story world. Yet it is important to note that in the narrative itself the two major conflicts overlap and interweave,[29] each one anticipating and paralleling the other at key points, and each illuminating the other by comparison and contrast. Furthermore, all of those in conflict with Jesus share similar traits. The demoniac forces, the authorities, and at times the disciples dominate people, oppose Jesus, put him to the test, are afraid, and are preoccupied with saving themselves.[30] The narrator suggests these similarities by means of verbal threads, parallel actions, and the juxtaposition of episodes. That is, the narrator has interwoven all the conflicts into an artistic whole so that one conflict is to be seen in relation to the others. As these conflicts merge in a dramatic climax in Jerusalem, there is a sense in which the primary opponent becomes death itself.[31] In this way, the resolution comes to focus on the characters and the different ways they deal with the threat of death. This observation leads us directly to a consideration of the Markan characters.

5

The Characters

Characters are a central element of the story world.[1] An analysis of the characters in Mark's story inevitably overlaps with the analysis of the conflicts, since the characters are so integrally related to the plot. Character analysis deals in part with the actions of a character in the plot of a story.[2] Yet characters are memorable apart from the plot and deserve to be dealt with separately; after all, we recall Hamlet and Huck Finn as we recall real people, not just as elements in a plot. Thus, we can analyze not only what characters "do," but also who they "are," treating them as autonomous beings and assessing them as we assess real people.[3]

In Mark's story Jesus is of course the dominant character. In addition, the authorities can be treated together as a single character, because the different groups which oppose Jesus share similar traits and carry on a continuing role in the plot in relationship to each other.[4] For the same reasons, the disciples also can be treated as a character. And although Peter, James, and John have individual roles, they typify the disciples as a whole. The minor characters, whom we call the "little people," can also be treated together because of their similar traits. They should not be dealt with as a single character since they have no relation to each other in the development of the plot.[5] John the Baptist and other character-agents, such as God and Satan, have been treated briefly in earlier chapters.[6]

Characterization refers to the way a narrator brings characters to life in a narrative. The narrator "tells" the reader directly what characters are like. Or the narrator "shows" the characters by having them speak and act and by having others talk about them and react to them.[7] The narrator of Mark's gospel primarily shows the characters to the reader rather than telling about them. The narrator reveals characters by evoking pictures, suggesting images, to the reader. As the story unfolds and the characters are gradually revealed, the reader has the initial impressions confirmed or adjusted or overturned.

The narrator of Mark's story uses many methods in characterization. In an earlier chapter, we saw how the narrator of Mark's story established some characters as reliable and others as unreliable by the use of an aside to the reader, or by the manner of their introduction into the narrative, or by an inside view of the characters' thoughts and feelings. The narrator also leads the reader to measure the characters against the standards of judgment in the story, which are primarily established through the teaching of Jesus.[8] In addition, the narrator reveals characters by comparison and contrast with other characters in the story, partly through the framing device but also, as we shall see, by other means. Finally, irony is a predominant means for revealing character in Mark's story. In these and other ways, the narrator also controls the reader's distance from or identification with characters in the story.[9]

The reader grasps and assesses these characters by interpreting the whole characterization. That is, the reader reconstructs what kind of "persons" the characters are in the same way that we evaluate people, observing what they say and do and how others react to them. The reader also takes note of the characters' participation in the events of the story, their interactions with others, the motives assigned or suggested by the story,[10] the ways in which the characters live up to the standards of judgment in the story, and how they compare with other characters. From these, the reader reconstructs a character such as Jesus, determining his personal traits, his values and world view, his attitudes, struggles and motives, the dynamics of his relations with others, the integrity of his words and actions, his development as a character, and so on.

An important part of this reconstruction manifests itself in the assigning of traits to a character.[11] A trait is defined as a personal quality of a character which persists over the whole or part of the story. The reader will find some traits named in the narrative and infer others from the characterization. For example, Jesus appears as "authoritative," "clever," "harsh," "enigmatic," and so on, while the authorities are defined as "defensive," "self-serving," and "afraid." We may also evaluate how the traits of a character relate to each other and determine which of the traits predominate over others. Literary critics refer to a character who has changing and conflicting traits, who is complex and unpredictable, as a "round" character. By contrast, a "flat" character has fewer, usually consistent, traits and is generally predictable. A "stock" character is completely flat, having only one trait.[12]

In modern novels, characters are often dynamic, changing and developing with a consonant transformation of personal traits. In Mark's story, the characters reflect some but not a great deal of change and development. The narrator, however, reveals the characters gradually so that the readers' perception of the characters changes and develops. Events and conflicts bring out the traits and true selves of the characters. As the plot develops and moves to a climax, the major characters are shown fully for who they are in the face of death. The narrator of Mark's story cleverly reveals the characters in such a way that the readers are constantly expanding or shifting their impressions of those characters as the story develops.[13]

JESUS

By announcing in the first line that Jesus is "the anointed one, the son of God," the narrator establishes Jesus as the central, heroic figure of this story.[14]

Characterization. The narrator creates a very complex characterization of Jesus. What Jesus *says* discloses his understanding of himself and his purposes. What Jesus *does* reveals primarily the extent and nature of his authority from God. Both what Jesus does and says determine his values and the dynamics of his relations with other characters. They also show Jesus' integrity in living up to his values and commitments. What *others say* about Jesus includes a variety of reactions: God and the demons know him as son of God; his family considers him to be crazy; the authorities view him as a blasphemer, a criminal, and as one possessed by an unclean spirit; the crowds see him as John the baptizer raised or Elijah or a prophet; and the disciples eventually identify him as the anointed one, but do not grasp what it means. The centurion is the only human character who calls Jesus a son of God; yet given his limited role, he is not depicted as necessarily grasping the full implications of his words. Other reactions to Jesus include fear, offense, amazement, fierce loyalty, and determined opposition. Thus, what others say and how they react reveal the unusual, enigmatic, and controversial aspects of this character.

The narrator consistently maintains a favorable point of view toward Jesus. This favorable characterization leads the reader to align with Jesus; yet the awesome, mysterious, and demanding aspects of Jesus' character keep the reader at a distance and make it difficult for the reader to identify easily with Jesus. Though the reader "aligns" with Jesus, he or she still "identifies" with some of the reactions to Jesus on the part of other characters.

Jesus is a "round" character, not in the sense of having conflicting or changing traits, but because those traits are many and varied, creating a rich characterization. The key to Jesus' character lies in the disclosure that he is the human being given authority by God to establish the new order of God's rule in the midst of a hostile and uncomprehending world. The narrator portrays him as a man of powerful action who impinges everywhere on the world around him. Because of his authority, he is awesome and frightening, as well as enigmatic and unpredictable. But because of the limits of his authority, he struggles and is frustrated. Because he does not dominate people or make direct claims for himself, he must lead people to understand by words and actions. He is often harsh, impatient, and angry. But he persists in his authority as healer and teacher and confronts oppressive forces wherever he goes, until in Jerusalem he submits to rejection and death in obedience to God. In this characterization there is an important dimension: Jesus is a person of integrity who lives out the standards of his own teaching.

The narrator shows Jesus' character developing as he struggles with the uncooperative people being healed, his popularity with the crowds, the rigidity of the authorities, and the hard-headedness of the disciples. Also, Jesus discovers, as a result of the faith of the Syrophoenician woman, that his authority extends beyond Israel, and that gentiles too will receive bread before the children of Israel are fully satisfied. And he makes a major shift in strategy when Peter identifies him as the anointed one, for after that episode Jesus moves quickly toward death in Jerusalem.

The narrator also gradually reveals Jesus to the reader, primarily by means of the literary motif of secrecy. The narrator's opening aside reveals Jesus to the reader as "anointed one" and "son of God," but these epithets do not tell what task Jesus is anointed for or what it means that he is God's son. These meanings unfold in the narrative as

Jesus struggles to fulfill his destiny and as other characters struggle to understand Jesus. As Jesus becomes known to other characters in the story, developments take place which lead readers to expand and shift their understanding of Jesus. At the end of the story, the reader sees the full meaning of Jesus' identity, but only through irony; it remains hidden to those in the story who are blind to him.

Jesus' authority. In Mark's story, Jesus is neither God nor a divine being, but a man who is given authority by God. He is a carpenter from Nazareth in Galilee, whose mother's name is Mary. He has numerous brothers and sisters. He becomes God's son at his baptism, for it is then that God declares Jesus to be the son and anoints him with the holy spirit. Jesus is sent in the same sense in which John the baptizer is sent, except that Jesus is empowered by the spirit and is given much more authority because it is his task to usher in a new order, the rule of God.

Jesus' whole character, in a sense, evolves from this formative experience. He is driven by the spirit and is single-minded in his efforts to act on God's behalf. Everything he does and says seems to issue from a conviction that through him "the rule of God has come near." As a result, he is both authoritative and determined. He is also confident and bold. As one anointed by God he assumes awesome rights and powers for himself—pardoning sins, interpreting laws, appointing twelve to share the authority, exorcising demons, healing, commanding nature, prophesying, entering Jerusalem royally, and occupying the temple.

Jesus is so powerful as to be frightening even to his disciples. And his feats of authority against all nonhuman powers that oppress people become more awesome as the story unfolds: from exorcising a demon, to cleansing a leper by touch, to healing by word alone, to commanding wind and sea, to healing those who touch just his clothes, to raising the dead, to providing bread for thousands in a desert. In short, "How well he does everything." And the astonishment of the other characters guides the reader to respond similarly.

Furthermore, Jesus fearlessly exercises authority over what is unclean.[15] Jesus counters the experience assumed by the society in the story world that uncleanness is contagious. Jesus' action with the leper shows his authority over the unclean: Jesus touches him, but instead of Jesus being defiled, the leper is made clean. His power is *holy* power in contrast to what is unclean. By the holy spirit, he exorcises unclean spirits. He calls toll collectors and sinners, heals a leper and the woman with a flow of blood, exorcises a legion of demons on gentile territory from a man who lives among graves and near pigs, raises a dead girl, and eats with a gentile crowd in the desert. Also, Jesus has authority to say, contrary to written laws, that what makes one unclean is not contact with unclean people or things, but evil and immoral behavior.

Jesus' authority includes prophetic wisdom and insight. He refers to himself as a prophet, and the crowds associate his activity with the ancient prophets. He announces the rule of God, calls for repentance and faith, performs prophetic actions of healing and exorcism which manifest God's present rule and foreshadow God's future complete rule, and proclaims God's will through riddles, prophecies, and interpretations of the writings. Jesus also prophesies the future, often in minor matters such as where to obtain a donkey or where to find lodging, but also in important matters such as the circumstances of his death or the events to take place after his death or the final establishment of God's rule. Sometimes he has perceptive insights about the thoughts or intentions of other characters, although generally the narrator depicts him as not knowing what other characters are thinking or what they will do. Moreover, Jesus pronounces prophetic interdictions asserting the extent of God's future penalties against those who blaspheme the holy spirit, cause stumbling, or eat up the houses of widows.

Jesus' authority from God resembles the royal authority a king exercises over national institutions. Jesus knows God's will in legal matters and acts on it with confidence, establishing the priority of some laws over others, nullifying certain written laws, condemning oral traditions, and disregarding religious traditions. His actions reveal how he applies the law in specific circumstances. At every point he interprets the law so as to serve people, as an expression of love for neighbor. Furthermore, he enters Jerusalem prepared as God's king to rule there, but not as a military conqueror for he rides on a donkey, a symbol of peace. He is aggressive and hostile toward the abuses in the temple, exercising the royal right to drive out those misusing it and declaring God's will for it to be a house of prayer for gentiles. Jesus' royal authority is of course rejected and he is executed.

The story, however, depicts Jesus as the one whom God will firmly establish in authority in the future. In the riddle of the vineyard, what distinguishes the son from the slave is that he is designated to inherit authority over the vineyard. Furthermore, a prophecy Jesus cites tells how, after his resurrection, the anointed one will sit on God's right hand while God puts his enemies down under his feet. And at the final establishment of the rule of God, within a generation of his death, Jesus will come in glory on the right hand of the Powerful One. Jesus' brief transformation on the mountain foreshadows the time when the son of man will come in the "glory of the Father."

There are, however, definite limits to Jesus' authority. Jesus knows or discovers these limits.[16] He is not God, for "God is one" and "No one is good except the one God." Jesus does not have authority to determine who will sit on his right or left in glory, nor does he know the exact day or hour when the end will come. As a brother to those who do God's will, Jesus too must submit to God; he cannot save himself, except in losing his life. In the course of trying to silence the people he discovers that he has no authority to impose himself on others, except by ordinary means. He cannot make people be quiet or heal someone when no faith is present or make the disciples understand or the authorities repent. Jesus struggles with these limitations at many points because they leave him frustrated and vulnerable.

The great extent and nature of Jesus' authority explains in part why he appears to others so awesome and unpredictable. People react to him with fear, amazement, or offense. There is a mysterious quality about Jesus and his actions which overwhelms others and makes it difficult for them to understand him. Even among those who favor him, no category of their thinking is adequate to explain Jesus. People identify him variously as Elijah, John the baptizer, one of the prophets, and the son of David. But Jesus' authority is greater than any of these. In the story world, the anointed one is given far more authority than the other characters expect him to have, based on their understanding of great figures from the past. The failure to understand this is what keeps the wisest legal expert from the rule of God. The story stresses that there is only one God, but that also there is another beside God, a human, to whom authority is due as lord.[17] Even David, Jesus points out, called the anointed one "lord" (in the lower case throughout our translation, in contrast to God as Lord). The extent of Jesus' authority as agent of God is related to his saying "I am" (the one chosen by God).[18]

Integrity. As the anointed one, Jesus is the exemplary figure who shows the way of God for all to follow. So it is basic to his characterization that Jesus has integrity, that he lives the values he teaches. As such, Jesus' actions illustrate and interpret his teaching, and his teaching explains his actions. We see this especially in Jesus' faith, as well as in his willingness to serve others and lose his life.

Faith. In the story, Jesus has extraordinary dependence on and trust in God. He leaves his job as a carpenter and breaks with his family, depending on God to provide food, houses, and family relations among those who receive him in his travels. Furthermore, Jesus' authority from God is not magical but interrelated to his trust in God. Jesus acts as the prime example in the story of how everything becomes possible for one who has faith (because he remains dependent on God, for whom all is possible). Healing, for example, requires faith not only of the person healed but also of the healer, for when the disciples do not have faith, they are not able to exorcise a demon. Jesus' faith to move mountains is what enables him to heal and do astounding works of power. Also, Jesus' prayers are related to his faith. Jesus teaches that when a prayer or request is made to God in faith it will be granted, and he tells the disciples that their failure to pray kept them from being able to perform a difficult exorcism. The repeated portrayal of Jesus at prayer reinforces the depiction of him as a person of faith.

The narrator portrays Jesus' faith as total submission to God's rule not only in terms of trust but also of obedience. At Gethsemane, Jesus prays to God about his death. Jesus acknowledges in faith that for God everything is possible, but that not everything is God's will. Jesus asks God to remove the cup, but he qualifies his request in favor of obedient submission; he asks that he himself do what God wants, even if it means his own death. It is this complete dependence on God for his own salvation which is the source of Jesus' courage to renounce himself, be least, and lose his life. In this prayer, the narrator shows Jesus in intimate relationship with God, even addressing him as "Abba" or "my Father." This relationship, whereby God gives such extensive power and authority to Jesus and Jesus relies so completely upon God, characterizes Jesus as "the son of God."

Serving and not lording over others. While faith and authority are the foci of Jesus' relation with God, other teachings point to the style of his relations with others. Jesus tells the disciples to be everyone's servant.[19] The servant analogy relates to the use of power. Jesus tells the disciples not to use their power like one who is in a position to lord over others and be served by them but to use their power like house servants or slaves who, without regard for status or reward, use their power only on behalf of others whom they serve.

Jesus himself serves others—from a position of strength, not weakness. That is, his authority comes from God, not the pressures of people. His first allegiance is to God; then he loves the neighbor as himself. So he has no need to lord over out of fear or to get others to serve him; and his commitment to serve is courageous, for he loses his life by so doing. So Jesus' idea of service does not become a matter of doing what others want him to do except insofar as it remains consonant with his understanding of God's will. He will heal others who request it, like Bartimaeus, but he will not grant the request of James and John who want power and glory. Strong-willed and independent, Jesus has a clear sense of his own mission, and neither traditions nor laws nor public pressure nor fear of indictment prevent him from speaking or acting.

The analogies by which Jesus depicts his own activity reveal how he serves people without lording over them. He describes his relations with demons as a violent action of binding the strong one and plundering his goods. But he depicts his relation with people as noncontrolling: The sower sows the word and has no control over the variety of responses, but "sleeps and rises," trusting God to bring growth and a harvest. (Just so, after Jesus finishes "sowing" the words of this riddle, he sleeps in the boat during the storm!) Similarly, in the riddle of the vineyard, the slaves and sons come to get produce from the farmers without using any violence. As one who serves, Jesus does not relinquish his authority, but leads like a shepherd whose care for the sheep is marked by compassion.

Jesus uses his great authority to serve people—liberating them from demons, illnesses, sin, uncleanness, and oppressive laws and traditions. Jesus' commitment to serve and not lord over is evident also in his *manner* of relating to people: the minor characters, the disciples, and the authorities.

Jesus serves the minor characters. He never tires in responding to requests for healing. In response to their faith, he heals readily. He even heals for the Syrophoenician woman when her great faith becomes apparent. He sees faith in people's persistent efforts to be healed, and where faith is weak, he encourages it. He even credits the person's faith or God's power, rather than his own authority, as the source of healing. Jesus forces healing on no one. He does not seek people out to heal but heals only those who come to him. He initiates a healing only when he takes responsibility for healing on the Sabbath. And Jesus heals freely, with no strings attached to those healings. He does not demand that people believe he is the anointed one (none do) or even believe in the Jewish God. He does not require a person to be morally good, and he interprets the desire for healing as an indication of repentance. Jesus does not expect to gain personally from healing, for he never asks anyone he heals to follow him. Usually he orders them, often harshly, to keep quiet or go home. They proclaim or follow on their own, and Jesus does not consider either action a condition for healing. Jesus not only serves, but in Jerusalem Jesus freely receives spontaneous acts of service from others.[20]

Jesus serves the disciples by being faithful and teaching without controlling their responses. He is loyal to them, never suggesting he will disown them. He is angry and impatient in his urgent efforts to teach them, and he refuses their requests for power. He corrects and warns them as he struggles to have them understand. He strives to prepare them for his absence. He gives them few assurances about the future, except that they can count on his continued commitment and the pardon of sins. And he respects their freedom to choose, using general conditional statements to affirm what is to be done or avoided: "If anyone wants to follow after me, he is to renounce himself" and "Whoever wants to be great among you will be your servant." He also teaches and leads by example, especially in the manner of his death. In the end, the narrator depicts him as not clinging to the disciples or trying to force their loyalty, for he dies without knowing all their future behavior or their ultimate fate. He dies out of his own obedience and entrusts the rest to God and the choices of the disciples.[21]

Regarding standards of judgment in the story, Jesus serves the authorities by confronting them, but without forcing *his* authority on *them*. In some scenes, Jesus is especially belligerent because he is opposing people who are oppressive. He tries to get his message across with explanation, often in spite of the threat of indictment. But he does not go to great lengths to convince them, letting his actions speak for themselves. He does not soften his words to please or appease the authorities but reveals their failures in relation to the rule of God, calling the Pharisees hypocrites and the high priests bandits, citing the writings against them and telling riddles against them. Jesus confronts the authorities with the nature of God's rule and with the seriousness of their offenses against it, but he does not impose his authority on them. After each confrontation, he moves on, leaving the authorities to choose their response. Even when he does use force, violently over-turning the tables and chairs in the temple, driving people out, and refusing to let anyone carry a vessel across the temple, he symbolically occupies the temple only briefly and then withdraws, leaving the high priests to respond to his action.[22] Likewise, his cursing the fig tree is a symbolic act against Israel for not bearing fruit in the presence of the rule of God.[23] He is not a military messiah who uses a sword or manipulates the crowds in an attempt to impose his authority. He does not even fight to defend himself, and he endures the consequences of his opponents' scorn.

Renouncing self, being least, and losing his life. The narrator portrays Jesus as submissive to the authority given him under God's rule and renouncing all personal claims to wealth, power, status, and even his own life.

Jesus never uses his power and authority to his own advantage. He does not curry favor with the crowds, and he even tells people to be quiet about healings, in part to play down his popularity with those crowds.[24] Although the crowd protects Jesus at times, he does not use the crowd to establish himself in a position of power.

The narrator portrays Jesus assuming great authority from God without making personal claims for himself. Jesus avoids saying that he is the anointed one and the son of God. This silence not only enables Jesus to avoid indictment, it also expresses the notion that it is not up to Jesus to make these claims for himself. It is for others to identify him.[25] He acknowledges his identity only when confronted directly with the specific confession by Peter and the specific questions of the High Priest. He uses the provocative "I am," yet only in contexts where it could also mean simply "It is I" or "Yes, I am."[26] Also, he refers to himself in the third person with the epithet, "the son of man." This self-designation unites many aspects of Jesus' role: the son of man who has authority to pardon sins and who has authority over the Sabbath is the same son of man who is scorned by the authorities and put to death; and this son of man who gives up his life for others will soon come in power to gather the chosen ones and be ashamed of those who were ashamed of him.[27] Thus, Jesus uses "son of man" not only to avoid indictment but also to affirm that from beginning to end he is a "man" who makes no personal claims and who depends on God for his authority and his glory.

The ultimate renunciation occurs when he gives up his own life. In a sense, Jesus meets all the standards of his own teaching in his death. His willingness to die expresses his total faith in God for his salvation. His death is the final act in a life of service and manifests his refusal to oppress others to save himself. And in this awful death—misunderstood, falsely accused, abandoned—he is least of all.

Jesus faces death. In the story, the portrayal of Jesus changes from the powerful one who relieves suffering to the vulnerable one who is the victim of suffering. The characterization of Jesus is basically the same at the end as at the beginning; it is a two-step progression in which the second step clarifies and makes the first step precise. This characterization is illustrated in its entirety by the statement that Jesus came "to serve, and to give his life a ransom for many." The difference between the first half and the second half of the story is the nature of the opposition and the kind of authority Jesus is given to deal with each. In the first half, he overcomes demons and nature by force; in the second half, he confronts human oppression.

Jesus is courageous and determined in facing his death. Jesus knows the inevitability of his death and moves inexorably toward it. The narrator even portrays Jesus as bringing on his death and cooperating with those who are responsible for it. Jesus invites the hostility of the authorities by going to Jerusalem to confront them, attacking the temple, and debating with them. Then, after his arrest in Gethsemane he becomes cooperative, does not resist arrest, volunteers evidence for his death sentence, and refuses to defend himself before Pilate. No longer combative, he endures ridicule and death silently.

Jesus' encouragement and acceptance of his death is not, however, portrayed as his own desire. Rather, he invites this kind of death because of a conviction that it is necessary; God wills it, and therefore it must happen so the writings might be fulfilled. Although he sees the necessity for it, Jesus still fears it. At Gethsemane, Jesus wrestles with his fear by facing it squarely. The narrator portrays his fear as an agonizing inner struggle, for Jesus does not want to die. The narrator depicts him as alarmed and anguished, "sad to death," as he prays that he will not have to die; yet he prays three times to submit to God's will. Finally because he subordinates his will to God's, he faces his approaching death without resisting his captors or lashing out at subsequent abuse and ridicule. Beyond this he experiences the full pain of crucifixion without relief from drugs or wine.

The narrator reinforces the inevitability of Jesus' suffering and death by a rhetorical device which creates suspense.[28] At numerous points, the narrator leads the reader to think Jesus might escape his fate: Jesus asks God to take away the suffering; someone raises a sword to resist arrest; the high priests cannot get witnesses whose testimonies agree; Jesus is silent; Pilate favors Jesus; the crowd gets a chance to ask for Jesus' release; the sun grows dark (earlier, in Jesus' prophecies of the end, darkness had signified God's impending deliverance); Elijah might come to take him down. Although the reader has heard Jesus prophesy his death, the reader still is led, time and again, to hope that Jesus might escape this fate. But each time, the raised hope is quickly dashed by some development in the plot. The impending death moves swiftly to a conclusion, when the narrator says: "And Jesus, letting out a loud cry, died." There is to be no reversal, no deliverance from this suffering. God really does abandon Jesus to his death.

The meaning of his death. The narrator portrays Jesus as believing that his death has meaning, an act of service which is "a ransom for many." That is, Jesus sees his death as the sacrifice by which God renews the covenant with Israel to include the "many," namely, Jews and now gentiles alike who respond positively to the rule of God in Jesus. Throughout the story, there is a transition from the ancestral community of Jews to a new grouping comprised of those who see the rule of God in Jesus. Jesus' family now includes those who do the will of God by following Jesus, and those who have the mystery of the rule of God are distinguished from those on the outside. Jesus sees his death as the crucial turning point for this transition. He understands his death at once as the point in time when the traditional community will seal its own destruction by rejecting him and also as the point when a covenant reestablishes the people of God. That is, because the farmers kill the heir, they will be destroyed and the vineyard given to others. Also, the temple which ought to have been a house of prayer for gentiles will be pulled down, and the stone which the builders rejected (referring to Jesus) will become the cornerstone of a people which includes gentiles. At the Passover meal, Jesus refers to "my blood of the covenant which is about to be poured out for many." Covenants require a blood sacrifice. Jesus sees his death as that ransom, not in the sense of a price to be paid to God but as the sacrifice necessary to seal this covenant for "the many."[29]

The "many" who respond to the good news will comprise the new temple not made with hands. They will pray in faith wherever they are and depend on God's pardon as they pardon others, considering love for God and neighbor more important than offering sacrifices. In Jesus' absence,[30] they will follow him by being like him, acting in his name, and proclaiming among the gentile nations as he proclaimed in Israel. The Jewish authorities had failed to bear Israel's mission for the gentiles. Jesus believes that their rejection of him will result in the sacrifice by which God will bring his rule to include gentiles.

The narrator recounts events at the crucifixion which confirm Jesus' understanding of his death. God rips the temple curtain, sealing its destruction and the destruction of the traditional Jewish community. Foreshadowing the new ordering of God's people are a gentile (the centurion) and a Jew (Joseph of Arimathea) who respond favorably to Jesus' death. The key to this reordering of God's people is that they "see" the rule of God in Jesus, especially in his death. While the authorities are blind to this, the centurion sees how Jesus dies and says, "this man was a son of God."

Similarly, the narrator wants *the reader* to see God's ruling king in this dying man. The narrator uses irony to draw the reader into this insight and at the same time to reveal Jesus' character. The crucifixion scene is portrayed in one way, yet it signifies the opposite. Everything the opponents say is mockery, but the narrator intends the reader to see the opposite: what they say in derision is true. Jesus is enthroned with one on his right and one on his left. The charge reads: THE KING OF THE JEWS. He wears a crown woven from thorns, and those who jeer him call him king. Earlier he was dressed in purple and his tormentors gave obeisance to him. The mockery is ironic testimony to the true kingship of Jesus as he hangs in agony; God's rule is triumphant in Jesus' death. Everything in the scene exemplifies what the rule of God is about; but God's rule is hidden, except to those who think "the things of God."

Thus, Jesus' death is the supreme moment of illumination in the story. The narrator leads the reader to see in it the ultimate paradox of God's rule, that the anointed one is king not in spite of but precisely because of his loss of life for others. Only when Jesus has "died like this" does the narrator allow a human character in the story to acknowledge Jesus as son of God, for it is by dying for the good news that Jesus fulfills his role as son of God. The meaning of Jesus' death for this story lies implicit in the centurion's statement of recognition, in the powerful way Jesus' act of sacrificial service transforms others, including the reader of this story, to see and follow.[31]

The death. At the opening of the story, Jesus—a man of action— powerfully impinges on the world around him. At the end of the story, the focus shifts to what befalls him, to what Jesus endures. The depiction of his death therefore maintains both a poignancy and a powerfulness.

Jesus faces death alone, for all his relationships fall away at the end This isolation of the hero, so typical of Greek tragedy, increases the pathos of the story. First, Jesus is betrayed by a disciple close to him. Then his disciples fall asleep at Gethsemane and his three closest companions cannot keep watch. When he is arrested, the disciples flee, and Peter renounces him. Removed from all support from followers, he is subjected to a trial by fellow Jews, characterized by false testimony and mockery. The subsequent trial before Pilate leads to his abandonment by the crowd. The phrase "handed over" conveys how vulnerable and helpless he is. He is handed over to hostile Jewish authorities, who in turn hand him over to the Roman official, who then hands him over to be crucified by foreign soldiers. Further abandonment is expressed when the soldiers divide up his clothes while he hangs on the cross, alive. Finally, Jesus' last cry attests to his abandonment by God. Jesus dies alone, and a stranger buries him.

The narrator also depicts another kind of isolation in Jesus' death. No one in the story understands him. His disciples and the crowds never fully comprehend what he is about. He alone has the conviction that he is doing what is the necessary will of God. His crucifixion as "king of the Jews," as we have seen, is an obvious occasion for ridicule, a source of taunting for the Roman soldiers and the bystanders, as well as the high priests and legal experts. Even those crucified with him join the ridicule.

Add to this the portrayal of physical anguish. They put hands on him and lead him off. Some of those convicting him spit on him, then cover his head and strike him. The guards beat him. He is bound and handed over to Pilate, who has him whipped. The soldiers spit on him and beat him over the head with a reed pole. After these beatings, Jesus is so weak that they draft someone to take up his cross. The agonizing crucifixion lasts six hours. The intensity of Jesus' suffering results in his quick death, for Pilate is surprised that Jesus has died so soon.

Until Jesus' cry of despair from the cross, the narrator has portrayed Jesus as a man who is confident in his understanding of God. On the cross, however (with a line from Psalm 22, of a righteous sufferer), Jesus cries out in isolation and despair: "My God, my God, why did you abandon me?" The narrator could have chosen to end Jesus' life on a note of triumph, but instead chooses an ending which makes this story compelling and profound. The narrator suggests by this stark ending that even though Jesus chooses to die in obedience to God, he experiences in death itself abandonment, doubt, and the uncertainty of what the ultimate meaning in all this is. Mark's narrative depicts the awesome nature of death. Death is abandonment. Death is isolation and separation. Death is the end. The narrator portrays Jesus experiencing the full impact of that death. And if there is to be anything after death, it comes through an act of God.

THE AUTHORITIES

The opponents in the story are Jewish and gentile authorities in Israel: the legal experts, the Pharisees, the Herodians and Herod, the elders, the high priests and the High Priest, the Sanhedrin, the Sadducees, the gentile soldiers and Pilate.[32] What the opponents have in common is that they are in positions of power and leadership. Because Jesus threatens their authority, they oppose him from the beginning. Apart from Herod, Pilate, and the High Priest, they oppose him only in groups. There are individual exceptions—a synagogue ruler, a legal expert, Joseph of Arimathea, and the centurion. But because they do not oppose Jesus, we do not consider them as opponents and we deal with them elsewhere as minor characters.

Characterization. We used selected clues to give a sympathetic picture of the authorities in the analysis of conflicts. Here we will discuss the authorities as the narrator evaluates them. The narrator paints the authorities in a consistently negative light from their first mention as legal experts who teach without authority. The narrator builds their characterization on their opposition to Jesus. What the authorities say involves primarily questions which imply accusations or aim at trapping Jesus. As for what they do, they primarily work at plotting the destruction of Jesus. Neither Jesus nor the narrator says anything favorable about them. And the narrator's inside views of their thoughts and feelings regularly distance the reader from the authorities. Apart from attributing a few favorable attitudes to Herod and Pilate, the narrator depicts the authorities as thoroughly untrustworthy characters.

The authorities are "flat" characters with a few consistent traits, traits which are in direct contrast to the values of the rule of God. The opponents have no faith, are blind to the rule of God, and are hardened against Jesus. Ironically, they think of themselves as guardians of God's law, but unknowingly they are God's enemies because their use of authority and their narrow legalism runs contrary to the way God rules. They are self-serving, preoccupied with their own importance, afraid to lose their status and power, and willing to destroy to keep them. As those who "think the things of men," they echo Jesus' depiction of the gentile great ones who "lord over" people. In the characterizations of the story, the authorities embody the opposite of Jesus and illuminate his character through contrast. Their presence in the story also highlights the failures of the disciples because of their similarity to the disciples.

The behavior of the opponents is consistent and predictable. As characters they do not change in the course of the story although the repetition of similar conflicts with Jesus enriches the reader's understanding of their traits. The full extent of their destructive mentality gradually emerges in their responses to Jesus' offensive actions and as a result of their frustrated efforts to get legitimate charges against him. Their opposition to Jesus broadens to include new groups of authorities, and their efforts to destroy him escalate until they execute him.

Blindness of the opponents. The opponents are blind to the rule of God. They have not been given the mystery that the rule of God is present; that is, they do not "see" that God's authority is behind Jesus' acts of exorcism, healing, and pardon. They require a "sign," yet do not see the signs given. Furthermore, Jesus' allegories about the rule of God serve only as obscure riddles to them. In Jerusalem, the blindness of the authorities seems most obvious in their ridicule of the dying Jesus; they will see and have faith only if Jesus miraculously gets down off the cross. Not only blind to the rule of God, the opponents are also blind to the wrongness and destructiveness of their own mentality.

Their blindness to the rule of God stems in part from their ignorance of the writings and of the power of God. The "legal experts" do not seem to know the legal precedents Jesus cites or the prophecies he quotes against them. They have no retorts for his legal arguments. In the world of the story, they also do not have the right understanding of God's plan, mistakenly believing that when Elijah comes he will first set everything right and that the anointed one will be a victorious military ruler, a son of David.[33] They do not know that it is necessary, according to what is written about them, for both Elijah and the anointed one to suffer and be rejected. Nor do some know from the writings the capacity of God's power to raise the dead or to establish the stone which is rejected. They are blind to the possibility that the writings could predict condemnation of them or that the power of God would bring destruction on them.[34]

Their blindness is closely related to the hardness of their minds. They become rigid in opposition to Jesus. They are deaf to his explanations or his defense of his actions based on the writings or his enunciation of legal principles, and their minds become further hardened against him. The word never penetrates them; "immediately Satan comes and takes away the word which was sown in them." As a result, they will not repent or turn and be pardoned. Because they cannot see God's active rule in Jesus, they have no faith about what is possible under the rule of God. The narrator portrays them as caught in a narrow legalism, a mistaken interpretation of the writings, and a misunderstanding of God, all of which, in the story world, results in a rigid mentality of destructive self-preservation. They really are on the outside, for they do not just passively fail to understand; they are hostile in their interpretations of Jesus' actions. They interpret his behavior as illegal and blasphemous. They accuse him of being possessed and of acting under authority of the ruler of demons. Thus, in a blind and fundamental opposition to Jesus and the rule of God, they become determined to destroy him.

By rejecting Jesus, they reject God. In the ancient world, actions against commissioned agents were considered actions against the one represented by those agents. Jesus' statement that "whoever receives me receives not me but the One who sent me" implies the converse: that whoever rejects him rejects not him but the One who sent him. This rejection is vividly depicted in the riddle of the vineyard where the farmers use violence against the son sent by the lord of the vineyard. The authorities' rejection of God becomes evident early in the story. By mistaking Satan for the holy spirit as the source of Jesus' authority, they repudiate God so fundamentally that Jesus calls this blasphemy against the holy spirit an eternal sin and affirms by prophetic oath that it will never be pardoned. Later at the trial, their condemnation of Jesus for blasphemy makes them guilty of blasphemy against God. In their blindness and rigidity, the authorities reject Jesus and his proclamation of the rule of God and, in so doing, unknowingly also repudiate God.

The authorities "lord over" people. The authorities were originally given authority in the vineyard (Israel) but have misused it to their own advantage. They do not bear fruit for others, nor do they take care to share with God what fruits they bear in the vineyard.

The story reveals what fruits they fail to produce. The leadership these authorities offer in Israel evolves in the story as the opposite of leadership that is appropriate to God's rule. For example, they do not share the compassionate concern for people that marks authority in the rule of God. They are not amazed that a cripple can walk, nor are they eager to see a man's withered hand restored, nor do they bring people to Jesus for healing. In their zeal to guard the law, they do not see the good Jesus does, nor do they themselves do good for people. As authorities, they do not interpret the laws to benefit people, but consider that laws have a priority and that people are made to follow the laws. So people are not to pick grain on the Sabbath when hungry or work on that day to save a life. Yet the authorities themselves go off on the Sabbath to plot with Herodians how to destroy Jesus. Also, they nullify the divine ordinances about honoring parents in order to establish their own traditions, the teachings of men. And they interpret the marriage laws loosely to the neglect of God's original intention in creation. Their legal interpretations either thwart acts of good or bring about harm.

They differ with Jesus' constitutional principle of legal interpretation, namely, to "love God" and "love the neighbor as one's self." They view laws requiring whole burnt offerings to be more important than the law about loving one's neighbor. Their commercial activities, changing common money for sacred money and selling unblemished doves for sacrifice, are ostensibly meant to keep the temple pure, but actually prohibit the poor and the gentiles from praying there. In their distorted interpretation of the law the high priests have failed to bear the fruit which, in Jesus' view, the institution of the temple should bring forth.

The authorities use "traditions of the elders" to keep themselves clean by separation from those who are unclean. They do not eat with toll collectors or sinners and employ ritual cleansings as a safeguard against gentiles or unclean Jews. This separates them from the "sinners," who need a doctor, and blinds them to the real source of uncleanness, "inside the minds of men," where behavior which is immoral and destructive is spawned.

Thus, the opponents use laws and traditions as weapons to accuse, to exclude, to destroy others, and to protect themselves. They even go beyond the law in order to arrest without cause, hold a kangaroo court, use false witnesses, bring to Pilate more charges against Jesus than that one on which he was condemned, and influence the crowd in what was to have been a popular decision for the release of a prisoner.[35] Because of these attitudes and behaviors, they are unable to comprehend the anointed one as a servant who pardons sins or interprets the laws to serve people or touches and eats with the unclean. Nor can they conceive of an agent of God who uses no force, refuses to lord over people, and does not even save himself, but who serves and dies for the many.

The opponents save their lives. The essence of the depiction of the opponents lies in that they are self-serving; that is, they are preoccupied with preserving their power, their importance, their wealth, and their lives. The authorities are impressed with their own greatness. The worst of the legal experts are enamored with formal greetings and want the most important places at banquets and synagogues. For pretense, they offer long prayers. Similarly, Herod holds a banquet for his greatest men and the first men of Galilee. Throughout the story they are threatened by Jesus' assumption of authority and his popularity with the crowds. In the vineyard riddle, Jesus depicts them as wanting to kill the son in order to get his inheritance. Later, Pilate considers that the high priests handed over Jesus out of envy.

Their authority does not derive from God. Their fear and their need to please the people in order to preserve their own positions of power and importance prove the point. Their authority derives from people, not God, for the opponents do not speak truthfully, but defer to others and "look to the reactions of men." Five times in the Jerusalem episodes, the narrator emphasizes that the authorities are afraid to speak or act because of the crowds. In the end, they arrest Jesus at night by a deception. This same fear and deference is also characteristic of both Herod and Pilate. Although Herod considers John to be a just and holy man, he has John beheaded "because of the oaths and those reclining to eat with him." Although Pilate is amazed by Jesus and knows that the high priests handed him over out of envy, he has him executed in order "to do the satisfactory thing for the crowd." Their authority is "from men" and they "think the things of men."

To save themselves, the authorities ultimately[36] become destructive. The vineyard riddle depicts the farmers using violence to keep what they have. This riddle allegorizes the actions of the Jewish authorities in their determination to destroy Jesus. Yet Herod and Pilate are no better, for Herod executes John and Pilate executes Jesus.[37] In the story, all these acts of destruction result from the authorities' efforts to preserve their positions of status and power over the people.

At the crucifixion, the authorities—Jewish and gentile alike—ridicule Jesus for his weakness, his vulnerability, and his death. Their attitudes toward death in their ridicule of him are most revealing. The authorities go to great lengths to avoid suffering, death, sacrifice for themselves. They do not realize that death is in any way redemptive. They cannot imagine an anointed one who could not or would not choose to save himself. Losing one's life for others as a means to save it, renouncing oneself or one's status to become a slave or servant, refusing to use power to lord over others, all are alien to the authorities' way of thinking. In relation to the standards of the story world, the authorities are so far off base in their ridicule of Jesus' vulnerability and death, that they unwittingly and ironically attest to the true dynamics of God's rule and plan for the son. They also reveal their own blindness to their situation and to the ultimate condemnation which awaits them when the rule of God comes soon, in power.

THE DISCIPLES

In the story, the term "disciples" comes to refer to the twelve men Jesus chooses to follow him. At first only brothers from two families are called, then Levi (who does not become one of the twelve). Then Jesus summons and makes the group of twelve, all of whom are identified by name. From then on, the term "disciples" refers to these twelve. Simon, James, and John, to whom Jesus gives nicknames, form an inner circle of disciples. These three are the only disciples with individual speaking parts. Judas also stands out because he hands Jesus over.

Characterization. The narrator characterizes the disciples both favorably and unfavorably. What the disciples do tends to reveal their loyalty to Jesus as close followers and helpers. Yet many of their actions as well as most everything they say exposes their failure to understand Jesus or to be like him. Jesus therefore corrects, reprimands, and warns them. Likewise, the narrator's inside views of the disciples' attitudes and

122

emotions are negative. Often, although not always, they distance the reader from having sympathy with the disciples.[38] Thus, the narrator portrays the disciples as being on Jesus' side, yet failing in their role. The disciples are "round" characters because they have conflicting traits. On the one hand, they are loyal and courageous, with a capacity for sacrifice and enough fascination with Jesus to follow him. On the other hand, they are afraid, self-centered and dense, preoccupied with their own status and power. They struggle to follow Jesus faithfully, yet they have many conflicting hopes and fears. They succeed in becoming fishers for men, but fail to meet other standards for discipleship set by Jesus. The depiction of them as "thinking the things of men" is a major means by which the narrator leads the reader to judge them negatively.

The narrator develops the disciples' characterization, in part, by contrast and comparison. The disciples are foils for Jesus in their failure to respond appropriately to the rule of God. In fact, their failures constitute the primary literary device by which the narrator reveals Jesus' standards for discipleship, for much of his teaching comes in the course of correcting their behavior and attitudes. Their contrast with Jesus is sharpest when, by use of the framing device, the narrator places Jesus' trial and Peter's denial side by side. The narrator also develops parallels between the disciples and the authorities, for although the disciples side with Jesus, they often reflect the mentality of opponents. Shortly we will see how the disciples fare in contrast to the many minor characters.

The character of the disciples emerges in response to the amazing experiences they have with Jesus and in reaction to his demands on them. As their character emerges, the readers' experience of the disciples changes.[39] The disciples are at first introduced favorably by means of their identification with Jesus. However, when they begin to speak and the narrator offers inside views, the negative traits become apparent and the readers are led to alter their initial impression. The first series of three episodes about the disciples favorably depicts them becoming fishers for men. Yet overlapping this series are the three boat scenes and three bread scenes. They also resist hearing Jesus' three predictions on the way to Jerusalem. After this shift in depiction, the disciples do change somewhat: they overcome some of their blindness when they accurately identify Jesus as the anointed one; they resolve their resistance to his claims that both he and they are to suffer; and they enter Jerusalem committed to follow him to death.[40] Finally, however, they abandon him at the point when discipleship confronts them with the prospect of death. The positive characteristics in the disciples, as well as some sympathetic inside views, maintain the reader's interest in hopes that despite their failures, the disciples will succeed in becoming faithful followers of Jesus.

Loyalty. Mark's story portrays the disciples as devoted to Jesus. They fulfill his promise by becoming fishers for men, leaving jobs and family to follow, going to him on the mountain when he commissions the twelve, then proclaiming, exorcizing, and healing when he dispatches them. They also regularly follow his instructions: they go when he summons them, take him in the boat, protect him from the crowds, assist in the desert feedings, find a donkey for him, and prepare the Passover meal. And they go with him anywhere he permits them, staying with him despite storms, trips to the desert, corrections, warnings, and little or no praise or assurance of reward. Even at the end, after he stresses repeatedly that they can expect persecution by following him and can expect no special rewards, they proclaim their allegiance to him until death.

Lack of understanding, lack of faith, and fear. Yet the disciples have great difficulty being true disciples. They are overwhelmed and frightened by Jesus, for instance. They are not enemies of Jesus, nor do they interpret his actions as hostile; rather, they simply do not grasp the significance of what is happening. They do not understand the riddles about the rule of God, even after Jesus explains them. The disciples do not even understand the significance of many of their own actions in light of the rule of God: not maintaining a pattern of fasting, eating with sinners, picking grain on the Sabbath, and eating with defiled hands. It remains for Jesus to explain each and to defend their actions to the opponents; and in at least one instance (defiled hands), they do not even understand his explanation. Also, they do not grasp the possibilities available through faith in the rule of God, such as stopping winds, providing food in a desert, or walking on water. They perform exorcisms and healings, but they are overwhelmed by everything beyond these. And they do not learn from one experience to the next. Nor do they know what these phenomenal experiences of faith on the sea or in the desert have to say about Jesus. For half the narrative, they do not know that Jesus is the anointed one.

Throughout the narrative, the lack of understanding surfaces as due in part to their fear and lack of faith. In the storm episode, the narrative parallels their fear with their lack of faith, both of which manifest their inability to grasp Jesus' identity. Elsewhere, their lack of faith keeps them from comprehending the meaning of the desert feeding, which in turn leaves them terrified when Jesus walks on water. Their fears and concerns about themselves on the sea and in the desert narrow their focus, so they cannot see what is really happening.[41] The climax comes in the third boat scene, which is also the third scene about bread, a combination underlining the extent of their failure to understand.[42] The disciples are once again anxious about bread because they have only one loaf. Once more they do not understand the power of faith. And they have not understood what the signs in the desert mean about Jesus and about the rule of God. In exasperation Jesus accuses them of being blind and deaf, with hardened minds. At this point Jesus' disciples differ little from his opponents.

Resistance to death on the journey. Then Peter identifies Jesus as the anointed one and the conflict shifts. Further traits of the disciples surface, not over the issue of Jesus' identity but about what he is going to do. He is going to suffer and die, and they are expected to follow his example. The disciples resist Jesus' new teaching at every point. Despite Jesus' warnings about the rule of God coming in power and despite the voice of God telling them that *this* one (Jesus, rather than Elijah or Moses) is the son[43] and that they are to listen to Jesus, the disciples persist in their resistance to death.

On the way to Jerusalem, Jesus predicts his death three times, and each time the response of the disciples is a dramatic denial and avoidance. Jesus says he will die, and Peter rebukes him. Jesus repeats his prediction, and the disciples argue about who is greatest among them. He predicts a third time, and two disciples ask for positions of power in glory. In response to Jesus' talk about losing their lives, the disciples become preoccupied with their own importance, seeking reassurance that their hopes for power and status will be realized. Their responses reveal that they followed Jesus hoping for power, wealth, and status, certainly not suffering. On the journey they are also exclusive and domineering, trying to stop an exorcist "who isn't follow-ing us" and rebuking people who bring children to Jesus for a blessing. Furthermore, they are astounded that an honest and prosperous man will not be saved. And when James and John ask for positions of power on the right and left, the other ten become angry. The disciples cope with Jesus' talk about death by clinging to their personal hopes and values.

This discovery about the disciples leads the reader to reevaluate their earlier behavior. The reader observes that the disciples followed Jesus in part because of the lure of becoming "fishers for men" and that Simon and the others were enamored of the crowds who were seeking Jesus in Capernaum. Until Jesus raised the possibility of rejection and persecution, the issue of the disciples' desire for importance did not surface. But when Jesus began to talk about rejection and death, the disciples evidenced how much they had expected glory and power.

Thus, what emerges in the face of Jesus' talk about death are the values of the disciples, which Jesus calls "thinking the things of men."[44] They want to acquire the world, be great, be first, and have power over others. And these desires underlie their destructive behavior, such as being competitive, self-centered, exclusive, and lording over others, all typically human attitudes and behaviors which the story depicts as different ways of saving one's life. These traits of the disciples emerge in stark contrast to Jesus' pronouncements about renouncing self, los-ing life, taking up a cross, accepting children, receiving the rule of God like a child, being like a slave or a servant, being least, giving one's money to the poor, and not lording over others, all attitudes and behav-iors which the story depicts as different ways of losing one's life for Jesus and the good news. The disciples' resistance to Jesus' teaching runs very deep, for even when James and John are finally willing to suffer like Jesus and drink the cup he is to drink, they want to do so only if they can be assured of positions of power and glory with Jesus! Their request therefore emerges as an attempt to manipulate the things of God in order to acquire the things of men. The hopes and expecta-tions of the disciples reflect their ways of dealing with the fear of death.

The disciples' fearful concerns about themselves derive from the root inability to grasp what Jesus is teaching them. It is no coincidence that the narrator frames the journey to Jerusalem with two healing stories about blindness, for the journey surely seems dominated by Jesus' urgent efforts to deal with the disciples' blindness to the things of God. Just before the journey begins, Jesus heals a man of blindness by touching him twice, after which the man sees everything clearly. This story may parallel the second touch the disciples now need to overcome their blindness. At the end of the journey, the blind Bartimaeus is healed and then "follows Jesus on the way." Perhaps this suggests too that the disciples now see clearly enough to follow Jesus to Jerusalem.

Fear and misperception in Jerusalem. It is not clear how much the disciples understand as they enter Jerusalem. In minor ways, earlier problems continue. They still express surprise at what is possible by faith in God when Jesus curses a fig tree. The size of the temple and the greatness of its stones impress them. Yet their verbal opposition to Jesus' death as well as their own disappears. They also cease talking about their hope for power and glory from a martyr's death. They seem willing to follow Jesus on his terms, for they have come to Jerusalem determined to be loyal to him unto death.

In these climactic scenes in Jerusalem the disciples still do not seem to understand their own human frailty in the face of death. They have misperceived again. They have not fully realized how threatening death is, nor have they prepared themselves for Jesus' arrest and separation from them. They are convinced that they can maintain loyalty to Jesus. So when Jesus says that one of them will hand him over, each asks incredulously "Surely not I?" And when he says they will all stumble, they protest vehemently that they will die with him rather than renounce him. The words spoken by Peter and echoed by the disciples are couched in the strongest possible language: "Even if I have to die with you, I'll definitely not renounce you."[45] They do not perceive, however, that in the face of death the spirit may be eager, but "the flesh weak."

Consequently their underlying resistance to and fear of death continue. They sleep and do not face death like Jesus, who prays that the testing might not come while summoning the courage to face it. So when the hour comes, they flee.[46] Peter follows from a distance, but in the end swears that he does not even know Jesus. Peter, who earlier represented the disciples' recognition of Jesus as the anointed one, now represents the disciples' realization of their misperception and failure. In this poignant scene, Peter remembers Jesus' prediction and breaks down, sobbing. He could not be loyal, as he has so desperately wanted to be. When all other considerations are stripped away, the disciples' fear and their need to 'save their lives' prevail, for they are unable to face the consequences of association with and acknowledgment of Jesus.

Unlike the opponents, the disciples (apart from Judas) do not destroy Jesus to save their lives. They are not against Jesus. They fail at being *for* him. And, in a sense, those closest to Jesus fail the most. Peter, James, and John are privy to many things throughout the narrative—a resurrection, the transformation of Jesus, the private teachings about the future. Yet they let Jesus down more than the others because he has especially asked them to keep watch for him and they do not. Peter, as the central spokesman for the disciples on so many occasions, protests his loyalty most vehemently. Yet he falls the hardest.

The failure of the disciples is like those seeds which fall on rocky ground. This analogy is directly related to the nickname "Peter," which in Greek is the word for rock. "Rock" was the kind of epithet (similar to "Sons of Thunder") which might have been applied to warriors to depict their imperturbability in battle. The epithet leads the reader to expect strength and heroism from "Rock," but the interpretation of the seed falling on "rocky" ground suggests an opposite and ironic meaning of that name, unmistakably depicting Peter and the other disciples: "Yet they don't have root within themselves but are short-lived. When oppression or persecution comes because of the word, immediately they stumble." They have received the word, but it has not taken root. Peter tries to live up to the heroic possibilities of the name Jesus has given him but is unable to do so. The depiction is especially biting when Jesus reverts to calling Peter "Simon" at the first instance of failure in Gethsemane: "And Jesus said to Peter, '*Simon,* are you sleeping? Weren't you strong enough to watch one hour?'" Similarly, all the disciples share Peter's weakness; though eager to be strong, when persecution comes they stumble.

The narrator has depicted the disciples as afraid, with little faith or understanding, concerned to save their own lives, and preoccupied with their own importance. But how do these traits relate to each other? It would seem that their anxious concern for themselves and their lives underlies much of what they do.[47] Fear for themselves manifests itself in their anxieties about threats at sea and hunger in desert places. To them, preoccupation with greatness and power becomes a way of assuring life and of avoiding death. The narrow self-concern and the fear of death blocks their capacity to understand Jesus or the values of the rule of God. In the end, the disciples fail to prepare adequately for death by persecution. In their portrayal, the whole movement of the story leads to that question for the disciples: "What will you do when faced with death for Jesus and the good news?"

Judgment and sympathy. The narrator's characterization of the disciples leads the reader to develop ambivalent feelings toward them.[48] On the one hand, the reader may want to condemn the disciples because when the disciples are measured against the narrator's standards of judgment and Jesus' expectations, they fail repeatedly. On the other hand, the reader is led to care about what happens to them, for they follow Jesus and succeed in making some changes. And Jesus himself cares about what happens to them. Also, some of the inside views evoke sympathy for the disciples, as when they are awed by Jesus' authority over the storm or when they are frightened by his transformation on the mountain. The scene of Peter's denial is especially poignant, eliciting great disappointment as well as empathy from the reader. Thus the narrator leads the reader to face squarely the harsh failures of the disciples and also to care about them and about how they will fare in the future of the story world. The final episode of the empty tomb evokes the same ambivalent responses. The reader wants the young man's joyful message to be relayed to the disciples. Yet the narrator undercuts that response by abruptly recalling the disciples' failures through the depiction of the fear and failure of the women. The story guides the reader to judge the disciples but not to reject them. For their fate is still an open question, and the reader wonders how the disciples will fare in the future.

THE LITTLE PEOPLE

In contrast to both the opponents and the disciples, minor characters in the gospel consistently exemplify the values of the rule of God. The minor characters make brief cameo appearances and then disappear, yet the role of each is often quite memorable. Examples include characters such as the men who bring a paralytic to Jesus, the leper, Jairus the synagogue ruler, the Syrophoenician woman, the children Jesus embraces, the poor widow, and Joseph of Arimathea. The brevity of their appearances and, in most cases, their anonymity in no way diminishes their importance within the narrative. Taken collectively, their impact on the reader is unmistakable and profound.[49]

Characterization. The narrator consistently introduces the little people favorably by having them come to Jesus either to ask something of him or to do something for him. They are "flat" characters with several consistent traits which they share in common: a childlike, often persistent, faith; a disregard for personal status and power; and a capacity for sacrificial service. In the words of Jesus, they are the "little ones who have faith." Usually they have no status in society, such as the poor widow; or they risk their status in coming to Jesus, as Joseph of Arimathea does. Nor is it incidental, in this regard, that many of them are women.[50] The little people act with childlike humility either by turning to Jesus for help or acting in service for others. And their behavior generally expresses their faith. The role of each is enriched by the repetitious presentation of characters who express similar traits in different contexts.

As individuals, the minor characters do not play continuing roles in the events of the story. The narrator does not develop them as a "group character" like the disciples or the authorities.[51] Yet their characterization shifts as the narrative progresses so that different traits are emphasized as the story progresses. The narrator develops the little people in this way, as foils for the disciples and for the authorities and as parallels to Jesus.

Faith, being least, being a servant. The little people measure up to the standards of judgment which Jesus proclaims. In the first half of the story, they especially measure up to Jesus' opening call to "repent and put faith in the good news." When the four men lower the cripple through the roof for healing, the narrator tells us that Jesus "saw their faith." Faith is expressed here as observable behavior, which typifies characterization of many of the minor characters. The narrator depicts the act of coming to Jesus for healing as an expression of faith. Jesus himself almost never initiates a healing; instead, people come to him. Often, those who come bring someone else to be healed; for example, others bring the cripple, the deaf mute, and the blind man. Other characters come on someone's behalf: Jairus and the Syrophoenician woman each come on behalf of a daughter. The active faith of these surrogates counts for the faith of those who either are not able to have faith because of demon possession or who are not able to express their own faith by coming to Jesus without the help of others. Those who come to Jesus demonstrate their faith by their actions; they kneel before him and plead with him.

The obstacles which many minor characters must overcome to reach Jesus reveal the extent of their faith.[52] In the story persistence is an overt sign of faith: the leper overcomes the social and religious barrier of his uncleanness; the four men bypass the crowd by lowering the cripple through a roof; Jairus has faith in spite of those who tell him his daughter already died; the woman with the hemorrhage contravenes public strictures against women and against the uncleanness of her condition;[53] the Syrophoenician woman overcomes Jesus' unwillingness to heal gentiles; and Bartimaeus gains Jesus' attention in spite of the efforts of the crowd to silence him.

In all these examples, faith simply involves someone's desire to be healed and the persistent trust that, through Jesus or the disciples, God will heal. And this faith restores the person. Where faith is absent, as at Nazareth, people cannot be healed.

The little people also measure up to the standards of judgment which Jesus introduces later in the story: renouncing oneself, losing one's life, being least, and being servant. The Syrophoenician woman is a good example. Although Jesus refers to her, a gentile, as a little dog, she willingly lowers herself to the status of a dog in order that the demon might be exorcised from her daughter: "Lord, even the *little dogs down under* the table eat the *little* children's *crumbs.*" She is willing to diminish herself, renounce herself, be least, in order to serve her daughter. The poor widow, who in Jewish society had a very low social status, is similarly portrayed. By giving out of her need everything she has, her *whole living,* she "loses" her life in service to God. Her low status and the smallness of her gift suggest she does not give for recognition or reward; in fact, she is unaware of being watched. Even though she has no direct contact with Jesus, the story depicts her as exemplifying Jesus' teaching.

In the final scenes, in Jerusalem, the little people exemplify especially the teaching about being "servant of all." Earlier, Jesus served others. Now in his time of need, others serve him:[54] Simon the leper receives him in his house; a woman anoints him with ointment worth a worker's annual salary; Simon Cyrenean takes up his cross; Joseph takes his body from the cross and buries him; and a group of women go to the tomb to anoint him after his death. These actions are acts of service done for Jesus by people who courageously sacrifice or risk something—money or arrest or reputation—to carry them out.

Foils for the disciples. The role of the little ones shifts as standards of judgment emerge in the story. Faith, being least, and being servant are exemplified by these people *throughout* the story, but different characteristics are emphasized at different stages of the story. In the first half of the story, their faith is emphasized. In the central section of the gospel pertaining to the journey, the little people best illustrate losing one's life, renouncing oneself, and becoming least. In Jerusalem, the emphasis involves the little people serving.

The changing emphasis in the role of the little people is related directly to developments in the depiction of the disciples. At each stage in which the little people exemplify a particular standard of Jesus' teaching, the disciples are depicted as especially failing to live up to that standard: first faith, then being least, and finally sacrificial service. Thus, the little ones serve throughout as "foils" for the disciples.

Also, the way in which the little people are compared to the disciples changes as the story develops. In the first half of the story, the little people are models of faith in comparison to the disciples, but without any *direct* comparison. Then, on the journey to Jerusalem and early in Jerusalem, the story makes explicit the contrast between the little people and the disciples; that is, Jesus tells the disciples directly to follow the example of certain minor characters. Twice he tells the disciples to identify with children in their lack of status and social power. And he tells them not to emulate a wealthy man who refuses to sell his goods and give to the poor. Also, he points to slaves and servants as models for discipleship. And he summons the disciples in order to praise as exemplary the generous, sacrificial act of the poor widow. Later, he praises the woman who anoints him.

Then, in the last scenes in Jerusalem, the little people actually fulfill the functions expected of disciples. Because the disciples of John had buried John's corpse, the reader expects the same of Jesus' disciples. Instead, the little people do what might have been expected of the disciples: a nameless woman anoints him; Simon carries his cross; a centurion makes the faithful confession at Jesus' death; Joseph goes to Pilate, requests Jesus' body, takes it down, and puts it in a grave; and the women who have followed him are present at the crucifixion and buy spices to anoint him after the Sabbath.[55]

In contrast to the disciples, who disappear in flight, the little people are highlighted. The narrator brings them to the fore by naming them. Earlier in the story, Jairus is the only minor character mentioned by name. In the Jerusalem episodes, however, Bartimaeus, Simon the leper, Simon Cyrenean, Joseph from Arimathea, Mary the Magdalene, Mary the mother of James and of Joses, and Salome all are named. Even the woman who anoints Jesus stands immortalized because her deed of anointing will be recounted wherever the good news is proclaimed. This naming makes the little people personal and memorable to the reader and emphasizes that they achieve their full identity in acts of service.

Finally, we note that the comparison between the disciples and the little people illustrates within the story Jesus' assertion that the most important will be least and the least most important. In comparison to the little people, the disciples attain importance by virtue of being disciples; yet in the end they are least in their capacity to think and live "the things of God." The disciples misunderstand their role, viewing it in terms of power and status and survival, rather than service and self-renunciation. By contrast, in the end the little ones are truly great within the standards set by the story. Within the story, the least become most important. They do not replace the disciples, who are called to heal and proclaim, but in their humble roles they demonstrate true greatness in the rule of God.

Thus, the little people increasingly gain the readers' attention as the story develops. In this regard, a parallel to the whole story is achieved through the single episode in which Jesus summons the disciples to watch the poor widow. In the same way, the whole story leads the reader to see the world with different values, to notice the little people and to learn from them. In this regard, their role in the story comes to parallel that of Jesus, giving the reader other figures with which to identify and other characters in whom to see "the things of God." In a sense, the little people function as "Christ" figures in the story world.

Continuing discipleship. The little people exemplify the standards of the story in momentary opportunities in their daily lives, especially in the way they receive those who proclaim the rule of God. By contrast, continuing faithfulness in difficult circumstances is expected of disciples. Disciples leave possessions, travel from place to place, heal, proclaim, exorcise, and face persecution regularly. Both the little people and the disciples are to renounce self, be least, risk life, and serve, but perhaps in different ways. The one who receives the commissioned agents of Jesus by giving them a cup of water "will definitely not lose his reward." Yet such little people may not have to live "the things of God" in the ongoing, difficult circumstances of being a disciple of Jesus. This distinction explains the surprising behavior of the women at the tomb. Based on the general portrayal of little people, the reader expects that the women will not fail. These women had followed and served Jesus in Galilee, had come to Jerusalem and were present at the crucifixion, and were now going to anoint the body. But when something more is demanded of them, they fail. They are to "go tell," but their reaction is fear and silence. The women's response illustrates the gap between a situation when people respond to the good news in the course of their daily lives and a situation when continuing discipleship is expected in terms of being sent, proclaiming, being handed over, and possibly being put to death.[56]

Note on the crowds.[57] The essence of the characterization of the crowds in Mark's story is that "they are like sheep without a shepherd." Throughout most of the story, the response of the crowds to Jesus reveals their need and desire for a leader. They acclaim his power; they crowd around him in confined and open spaces alike and follow him in droves to the desert; they come from everywhere in and around Israel; and their presence in such large numbers protects Jesus from the threat of his family in Galilee and later from the threat of the authorities in Jerusalem.

Crowds with traits similar to those of the little people often respond to Jesus. They come to Jesus wherever he is—in cities, by the sea, in the desert places. They press on him to touch him. Some bring others to be healed, put them in the markets, and plead with Jesus to touch them. Crowds show persistence in getting to Jesus: one crowd runs after him from one town to another; another follows his boat around the sea; still another stays with him for three days in the desert.

As long as Jesus remains present, the crowds follow him, respond to his compassion and his power, and are "glad to hear him." But when Jesus disappears from the scene, when the shepherd is struck down, then the sheep are scattered. The crowds now become vulnerable to other, manipulative leadership; the high priests stir them up to ask Pilate to release Barabbas rather than Jesus.

The crowds reject Jesus at the end partly because they have not understood him. The crowds are awed by Jesus. But for the narrator, awe is not an adequate response to Jesus, for it implies a lack of understanding. In this story, loving God "with the whole intelligence" is crucial. The disciples must come to understand Jesus before they are prepared to follow. The lack of understanding keeps the legal experts from the rule of God. The crowds too, though not at first hostile to Jesus, see him only as John the baptizer or Elijah or a prophet or the son of David. They are glad to hear that the anointed one is greater than David, indeed is David's lord, but they do not realize that he will be rejected and put to death. In the nationalistic fervor of the Passover feast, the crowd chants for someone to bring in the "coming rule of our father David." When Jesus refuses to fight, submits to arrest, and does not defend himself before Pilate, the high priests are able to stir up the crowd to choose Barabbas. The crowd chooses someone who will fight. Jesus is a disappointment.

Despite the rejection of Jesus by *groups* of people, such as the crowds, the high priests, the elders, and the legal experts, there are always individual exceptions, like the woman who anoints him or Joseph or the centurion, who are open to the rule of God in the right way and who respond favorably to Jesus, even when he is not being the shepherd. It is with such individuals that the seeds sown among the crowds take root and "produce thirty and sixty and a hundred per measure."

Summary. As we reflect on the reader's initial impressions of Jesus, the authorities, the disciples, and the minor characters, we realize how the narrative enables the reader to see, through surprising twists and turns, just who the central characters are. Appropriately to Mark's story, the characters are led in the end to a crisis over the issue of death; this story elucidates a God who expects people to "love God with the whole life" and "the neighbor as one's self." In the story world, this means dying for the good news, trusting God enough to lose one's life for others. So the ultimate test for the characters' responses to God must be how they will deal with death—and it is in the presence of death that the characters become fully known.

Conclusion

The author of Mark's gospel tells a dynamic story and has woven the tale so as to create powerful effects on the reader. We have been dealing separately with the various aspects of the story world and the rhetoric, but the reader experiences this story as a unity. He or she is drawn into the world of these fascinating people, strange places, and dramatic events—guided throughout by the omnipresent narrator. In this brief conclusion we want to weave some pieces of the fabric of our study together by discussing the reader's overall experience of this story.

Implied reader. We have mentioned often how the narrator leads the reader to respond in certain ways to different aspects of the story world. In each case, the "reader" we referred to is not an actual reader since it is not possible to predict the responses of an actual reader. Rather our reader is a hypothetical "implied reader," an imaginary reader with the ideal responses implied or suggested by the narrative, experiencing suspense or feeling amazement or sympathizing with a character at the appropriate times.[1] The implied reader is properly an extension of the narrative, a reader that the author creates (by implication) in telling the story. By reconstructing the hypothetical implied reader from the responses suggested throughout the narrative of Mark's gospel, we can identify some of the overarching effects this story might have on the reader.[2] There are several ways to focus the implied reader's experience of the story; we have chosen one for illustration.[3]

Our study suggests that the overall narrative leads the reader to see the hidden rule of God in Jesus and to follow him. First, the narrative leads the reader to *see*. The reader experiences a story world in which God's ways are hidden. Through Jesus, God inaugurates a new order of power and authority and a new set of relationships, but the characters must discern these as God's rule for themselves. However, the characters are so caught up in human ways of thinking that they cannot grasp God's ways. They are blind to the signs and do not have the categories to comprehend what is happening. God's rule calls people to trust God and renounce themselves so that they are liberated to serve others. But the characters in the story are mostly concerned with themselves, their own importance, power, and security, all of which prevent the authorities and the disciples from understanding Jesus' actions and teaching about God's rule. The conflicts which Jesus has with these blind characters reveal not only the depth of human resistance to renouncing one's life in order to serve others but also the extent of human destruction which results from saving one's life. Other aspects of the story also depict how God's ways are hidden to the world: the radical contrast between thinking the things of God and thinking the things of men, the characters' inability to recognize Jesus' identity, the obscurity of the riddles, the misinterpretation of the writings, the motifs of not seeing and not hearing and hardness of mind, and the prophecies of a time when all will behold the rule of God in power. By portraying a world in which many characters are blind to the hidden rule of God, the narrative leads the reader to want to see and understand.

While the story depicts characters who are blind to the rule of God, the rhetoric leads the reader to see God's hidden ways as well as to accept them. The reader knows Jesus' identity from the start and therefore has a context for experiencing Jesus' authority and for understanding his teaching. The rhetoric draws the reader into evaluating the characters as the narrator views them, marveling at Jesus' acts of power, sympathizing with Jesus against the authorities, and responding in sympathetic tension with the uncomprehending disciples. The first half of the story impresses the reader with Jesus' authority, knowledge, cleverness, and insight. By the midpoint of the story, the reader is so aligned with Jesus as to be much better prepared than the disciples to accept Jesus' new teaching that he and his followers are to renounce themselves, serve others, and lose their lives. And, as the disciples work through their own resistance to Jesus' teaching on the journey to Jerusalem—opposing him, questioning, asking for privileges—so also does the reader deal with possible resistance and misunderstanding. At the point in the narrative when Jesus arrives in Jerusalem, the reader has already seen what is involved in following the way of God and is prepared for the events to come. Then, through irony, the narrative draws the reader further into seeing the rule of God by seeing God's ruling king in the dying Jesus. Irony leads the reader to *want* to see, so as not to be like the blind victims of the irony of the story. And because of the standards of judgment which the story establishes, the reader accepts the acts of service and suffering on the part of the characters as expressions of true greatness.

Other rhetorical devices throughout the story also lead the reader toward sight and acceptance. The two-step progression leads the reader to look for further clarity. The many questions invite the reader to seek further understanding. And the framing device leads the reader to see the sacrificial service of Jesus and the little people in a sharp contrast to the cowardly, yet destructive behavior of the authorities and (sometimes) the disciples. In these ways, the story world and rhetoric together lead the reader to see God's hidden rule and to accept the true greatness of those who follow God's ways.

Secondly, not only does the narrative guide the reader to see and accept God's ways, it also leads the reader to *follow* Jesus. We have seen how the omniscient narrator enables the reader, in a sense, to be invisibly present in the scenes. In this way, the reader follows Jesus in his travels, gets involved in the conflicts, and identifies with the characters. And this movement of following Jesus leads the reader to deal with death; for the journey with Jesus ends in Jerusalem, and the conflicts move to a dramatic climax in death, and the characters only fully reveal themselves in that crisis. In addition, many of the rhetorical devices increase the reader's involvement through the story by pointing with suspense and tension toward these climactic events.

In the story dying for the good news—trusting God enough to lose one's life in service for others—is the basic expression of following God's way. The narrative leads the reader to be a faithful follower of Jesus by preparing the reader to face death. In the Jerusalem scenes, the reader sees all the characters dealing with death. By identifying with these different characters, the reader experiences the desire to save one's self, the avoidance of death, and the unwillingness to deal with the weakness of the flesh. But the narrator leads the reader to reject these, to identify and align with the hero Jesus, to want to be courageous as he is, and to want to have such faith in God's salvation as to relinquish one's own life in spite of one's fears and desires. Then through the powerful depiction of Jesus' death, the reader experiences vicariously the isolation, the pain, the rejection, and the despair of death. By facing death vicariously through the story, the implied reader is purged of some of the fear of death and is therefore better prepared to be faithful as Jesus was.

In summary, then, the narrative defines the implied reader as a faithful follower of Jesus.[4] The implied reader travels the journey with Jesus, like a disciple who understands the ways of God when others do not, accepts Jesus' teaching when his disciples resist, and arrives in Jerusalem prepared to go through death with Jesus. In a sense, by staying with the story, the reader remains faithful to the end, staying awake at Gethsemane, being present at the trial and crucifixion, and afterward following the women to the grave. Based on Jesus' earlier prophecies, the reader expects the grave to be empty but does not expect the surprising flight and silence of the women. This abrupt ending, which aborts the hope that someone will proclaim the good news, cries out for the reader to provide the resolution to the story. The reader alone has remained faithful to the last and is now left with a decision, whether to flee in silence like the women or to proclaim boldly in spite of fear and death. The implied reader will choose to proclaim.

A first-century reader. We can further illuminate the story by speculating on the responses of a first-century reader, for such an actual reader would have seen the events of the story world in relation to the events of the real world at the time of writing.[5] When we speculate on a hypothetical first-century reader, the key question is: "What actual reader are we talking about?" The story might have been heard by a Roman soldier, a Syrian peasant, a Jewish nationalist, or a moderate Pharisee, and each would have reacted quite differently. Even among followers of Jesus, some might have accepted the depiction of him as miracle worker but rejected the notion that his suffering was necessary. Other followers of Jesus might have been deeply moved by the portrayal of Jesus' death and might have resolved to be courageous in living out the new order brought about by God's rule.

This last reader, a sympathetic reader, would have responded to the story in much the same way as the implied reader and also would have had additional responses in light of the historical situation of the time.

Mark's gospel was probably written around the year 70 of the Common Era, at the end of a four-year war between Israel and the Roman Empire in which Israel was defeated, Jerusalem destroyed, and the temple ravaged.[6] At this time, some forty years after the death of Jesus, Jewish and non-Jewish followers of Jesus alike were troubled by this catastrophic event. The followers of Jesus expected him to return within a generation, and some may have expected him to appear at the temple in Jerusalem. They would have wondered what it meant that God's city and temple were destroyed and that Jesus had not yet returned. Perhaps Jesus had not really been the anointed one. Perhaps he would not return to establish the rule of God in power within a generation as they had expected.

The reader would be reassured by this story in which Jesus predicts all that has happened up to the reader's time—famines, wars, persecutions, the horrible desecration and destruction of the temple, and the appearance of many false prophets and anointed ones. Because these predictions had already been fulfilled in the real world, the reader would tend to trust Jesus when he says that the final establishment of God's rule and the return of Jesus were to occur, not at the time of the war or the desecration of the temple, but very soon after. The narrative also points the follower's hopes for Jesus' return away from Jerusalem toward Galilee and the gentile nations.[7]

Also, by telling a story about the immediate past, the gospel explains to the first readers the reason for the downfall of the temple and city. In the explanation offered by the narrative, the rule of God came with Jesus, and the Jewish leaders rejected this new order. They had not shared the fruits of the vineyard for generations, and by rejecting God's agent and condemning him to death they sealed their own destruction. At Jesus' death God departed the temple (signified in the story by the ripping of the curtain), leaving it to its destruction. The story implies that the destruction of the temple and the defeat of Israel by the Romans resulted from the authorities choosing the way of Barabbas over the way of Jesus. The destruction and the defeat are thus depicted as the consequent judgment by God on the farmers of the vineyard and the nation for pursuing policies of domination and control similar to those of the gentile rulers who lord over people, policies incompatible with the rule of God.

The first-century reader was also aware of the threat of persecution

141

to anyone who would follow Jesus—rejection by family, misunderstanding from Jewish compatriots, trials before local Jewish courts, and trials before gentile governors and kings. To the Jews, the followers of Jesus who opposed the war would have been viewed as traitors; to the Romans the followers of Jesus were suspected of revolution because their leader was executed as a revolutionary by a Roman procurator. Thus, if the reader were to act as the story suggests—proclaim the good news to gentiles before the end comes—he or she would have to face persecution and possibly death.

The overall impact of the story might lead this first-century reader, like the implied reader, to face death squarely and be better prepared to testify for Jesus and the good news of the rule of God. At the end, although disturbed by the fear and failure of the women, the reader still might choose to speak the good news boldly in spite of the consequences. And the reader's heroic efforts to live the values of the rule of God would be just as misunderstood and hidden to the world as Jesus' faithfulness was. But the reader would act in the conviction that very soon what is now hidden will be revealed and the son of man will come in glory to gather the chosen ones.

And what about the twentieth-century reader?[8] In one sense, the time-limits of the story world do not account for a reader beyond the generation of Jesus, because the story assumes that the rule of God will be fully established shortly after the temple is destroyed.[9] Nevertheless, the modern reader, having entered the story world and participated in it, can in many ways see our own society and our own lives reflected in the story, though from quite a different perspective. For in this world created by the author we have experienced the radical new order called for under God's rule, the possibilities of faith in God, the greatness of service for others, the destructiveness of dominating other people, the hidden power of redemptive suffering, the misuse of state and religion to achieve power and success, the potential blindness of religious commitment, the lure of a survivor mentality, the deep resistance to renouncing oneself and facing death squarely, the difficulty of choosing to be least, the courage of anonymous little people, the hardships of being faithful to the rule of God, and much more. Having experienced this story world, the readers may be able to see and struggle with the real world in new ways and perhaps be better prepared to live more courageous and humane lives.[10]

Notes

INTRODUCTION

1. Mark's gospel was probably written to be heard rather than read. It would, therefore, be appropriate to refer to the hearers of the drama. We have chosen, however, to deal with the gospel as literature and to discuss its readers. Therefore, some aspects of the text associated with oral narration will not be considered. See Thomas E. Boomershine, "Mark, the Story-teller: A Rhetorical-Critical Investigation of Mark's Passion and Resurrection Narrative" (Ph.D. diss., Union Theological Seminary, New York, 1974), pp. 7–9 and idem, "Oral Tradition and Mark" (Society of Biblical Literature, Markan Seminar Paper, 1979). See also Werner Kelber, "Mark and Orality," *Semeia* 16 (1979): 7–55.

2. Narrative is "an account in prose or verse of an actual or fictional event or a sequence of such events." See C. Hugh Holman's revision of William Thrall and Addison Hubbard's *A Handbook to Literature* (Indianapolis: Odyssey Press, 1972), p. 336. Our investigation into narrative includes what M. H. Abrams refers to as "objective criticism," which "describes the literary product as a self-sufficient world-in-itself" and "pragmatic criticism" (also called rhetorical criticism), which views the literary work as something "constructed in order to achieve certain effects on the audience" (*A Glossary of Literary Terms* [New York: Holt, Rinehart & Winston, 1958], p. 37).

3. For comprehensive introductions to the study of narrative, see, for example, Seymour Chatman, *Story and Discourse: Narrative Structure in Fiction and Film* (Ithaca, N.Y.: Cornell University Press, 1978); Wayne Booth, *The Rhetoric of Fiction* (Chicago: University of Chicago Press, 1961); Gérard Genette, *Narrative Discourse: An Essay in Method*, trans. Jane E. Lewin (Ithaca, N.Y.: Cornell University Press, 1980); Robert Scholes and Robert Kellogg, *The Nature of Narrative* (New York: Oxford University Press, 1966). Scholes and Kellogg deal with ancient narrative in *The Nature of Narrative*. Regarding ancient literary criticism, see especially Aristotle's *Poetics* and *Rhetoric*. On the verisimilitude of Biblical literature, see Erich Auerbach, *Mimesis* (New York: Doubleday Anchor Books, 1957).

4. Obviously, many commentaries and monographs on Mark have contributed much to a study such as ours which deals with Mark's gospel as a whole. Because of the focus of this study, however, we have limited the foot-note references primarily to works most relevant to the literary study of narrative, works from literary critics which seem relevant to a study of

Mark's story, and works by Markan scholars which deal with the Gospel of Mark as narrative.

5. Recently, Frank Kermode, writing on Mark, cautioned against finding too much unity in a text. Kermode writes that we are "programmed to prefer fulfillment to disappointment, the closed to the open," when in fact fractures and incoherencies in a text may "mime the fortuities of real life." See *The Genesis of Secrecy: On the Interpretation of Narrative* (Cambridge, Mass.: Harvard University Press, 1979), pp. 54, 64. John C. Meagher, in "Die Form-und Redaktionsungeschickliche Methoden [sic]: The Principle of Clumsiness and the Gospel of Mark," *Journal of the American Academy of Religion* 43 (1975): 459–472, argues simply that Mark was a (sometimes) careless storyteller who left many loose ends. We will not be in the best position to determine fractures in the Markan text until we have fully explored its integrity.

6. See Norman Petersen, " 'Point of View' in Mark's Narrative," *Semeia* 12 (1978): 97–121.

7. On closure in narrative, see Norman Petersen, "When is an End not the End?" *Interpretation* 34 (1980): 151–166. According to Petersen, closure refers to "the sense of literary ending derived from the satisfaction of textually generated expectations" (p. 152). Petersen is informed by Barbara Hernstein Smith, *Poetic Closure* (Chicago: University of Chicago Press, 1968) and Frank Kermode, *The Sense of an Ending: Studies in the Theory of Fiction* (London: Oxford University Press, 1966). For further bibliography on closure, see Petersen's article.

8. See Robert Tannehill, "The Gospel of Mark as Narrative Christology," *Semeia* 16 (1979): 57–92.

9. For discussion of the study of the gospel narratives, see Norman Petersen, *Literary Criticism for New Testament Critics* (Philadelphia: Fortress Press, 1978) and "Literary Criticism in Biblical Studies," in *Orientation by Disorientation: Studies in Literary Criticism and Biblical Criticism,* presented in honor of William A. Beardslee, ed. Richard A. Spencer (Pittsburgh: Pickwick Press, 1980). See also John Patton and Vernon K. Robbins, "Rhetoric and Biblical Criticism," *Quarterly Journal of Speech* 66 (1980): 327–350. Earlier, Norman Perrin had called for a study of plot and character in "The Evangelist as Author: Reflections on Method in the Study and Interpretation of the Synoptic Gospels and Acts," *Biblical Research* 15 (1972): 5–18. Many of his students responded with *The Passion in Mark: Studies on Mark 14–16,* Werner Kelber, ed., (Philadelphia: Fortress Press, 1976). See also Roland Mushat Frye's appeals for the use of "standard" literary criticism in "A Literary Perspective for the Criticism of the Gospels," in *Jesus and Man's Hope,* vol. 2, ed. Donald Miller (Pittsburgh: Pittsburgh Theological Seminary, 1971), pp. 193–221; and "Literary Criticism and Gospel Criticism," *Theology Today* 36 (1979): 207–219. See also David Rhoads, "Narrative Criticism and the Gospel of Mark," forthcoming in a 1982 issue of the *Journal of the American Academy of Religion.*

Notes

10. Scholars are uncertain about the author, date, and provenance of the gospel. An ancient tradition claimed that a certain Mark wrote down the recollections of Peter, though not in the right order. Tradition also associated the gospel with Rome. But many scholars today doubt the veracity of these traditions, and clues from the story itself weigh against them. In any case, these traditions are not decisive for interpreting the story. Scholars generally agree that the author wrote around the time of the Roman-Jewish War, 66–70 of the Common Era. Yet even this conclusion comes from correlating references in the story with events of history, a procedure that follows rather than precedes the interpretation of the story. On these important and controversial matters see, for example, Hugh Anderson, *The Gospel of Mark* (London: Marshall, Morgan, and Scott, 1976), pp. 24–32. In spite of the controversy over authorship, we will continue to refer to the author as "Mark."

11. Petersen, "Literary Criticism," pp. 21ff.

12. See Boris Uspensky, *Poetics of Composition: The Structure of the Artistic Text and Typology of a Compositional Form,* trans. Valentina Zavarin and Susan Wittig (Berkeley: University of California Press, 1973), p. 137. Petersen suggests that by entering the imaginative world of the work created by the author we may experience a second naiveté in relation to Biblical texts ("Literary Criticism," p. 2).

13. Petersen considers it a "referential fallacy" to view the statements expressed or implied in the narrative of Mark's gospel as a direct representation of the earlier historical events of Jesus' day. (*Literary Criticism,* pp. 38ff.)

14. In this distinction between "what" and "how," story and rhetoric, we are following Chatman, who prefers the word "discourse" to "rhetoric." See especially his helpful diagrams *(Story and Discourse,* p. 26).

15. For the integral function of "form" in Mark's narrative, see Boomershine, "Mark, the Storyteller," pp. 9–30, who observes that one should not view narrative as the mere vehicle for an idea.

1: THE GOSPEL OF MARK

1. We are grateful for the assistance of Professor W. F. Stinespring at the formative stages of this translation and for extensive help at other stages from Clifford Dull, Trudy Kastens, James Wilde, Larry Hurtado, Joanna Dewey, and Thomas Boomershine.

2. For an interesting effort to determine the proper pauses in the text between episodes, see David Noble, "An Examination of the Structure of Mark's Gospel" (Ph.D. diss., University of Edinburgh, 1972). Thomas E. Boomershine has worked out an episodic analysis based on an oral presentation of Mark's gospel. See "Mark, the Storyteller: A Rhetorical-Critical Examination of Mark's Passion and Resurrection Narrative" (Ph.D diss., Union Theological Seminary, New York, 1974).

3. With few exceptions we have followed the text of Mark's gospel in *The Greek New Testament*, eds. Kurt Aland et al. (Münster: United Bible Societies, 1975). We have not made reference to the many important textual variants. For example, throughout our study we assume that Mark's gospel ends at 16:8. See Bruce M. Metzger, *A Textual Commentary on the Greek New Testament* (London: United Bible Societies, 1971).

4. For example, we use both "restore" and "save" to translate the Greek word *sōzō* and "renounce" and "deny" to translate the word *aparneomai*.

5. For a fascinating translation of Mark's story which omits chapter and verse designations and reflects many elements of Mark's style, see Reynolds Price, *A Palpable God* (New York: Atheneum, 1978). See also the translation by Richard Lattimore, *The Four Gospels and the Revelation* (New York: Farrar, Straus & Giroux, 1979).

6. For example, we consistently translate the formula phrase "Amen, I tell you . . ." as a prophetic oath, "I swear to you. . . ." See George Buchanan, "Some Vow and Oath Formulas in the New Testament," *Harvard Theological Review* 58 (1965): 319–326.

2: THE RHETORIC

1. On narrators, see Seymour Chatman, *Story and Discourse: Narrative Structure in Film and Literature* (Ithaca, N.Y.: Cornell University Press, 1978), pp. 146–162; Wayne Booth, *The Rhetoric of Fiction* (Chicago: University of Chicago Press, 1961), pp. 149–163, and idem, "Distance and Point of View: An Essay in Clarification," *Essays in Criticism* 11 (1961): 60–79. For a collection of short stories illustrating various points of view with regard to narrators, see eds. James Moffett and Kenneth McEleheny, *Points of View* New York: New American Library, 1966). See also below, note 10.

2. On the narrator of Mark's story, see especially Norman Petersen " 'Point of View' in Mark's Narrative," *Semeia* 12 (1978): 97–121. See also Thomas E. Boomershine, "Mark, the Storyteller: A Rhetorical-Critical Investigation of Mark's Passion and Resurrection Narrative" (Ph.D. diss., Union Theological Seminary, New York, 1974); and Robert Fowler, "The Feeding Stories in the Gospel of Mark" (Ph.D. diss., University of Chicago, 1978), to appear in the Society of Biblical Literature Dissertation Series.

3. For an extensive list of the narrator's inside views into the thoughts of the characters, see Petersen, " 'Point of View,' " p. 22.

4. For a catalogue of such "stable" commentary by Mark's narrator, see Fowler, "The Feeding Stories," pp. 182–218.

5. On the use of "for" (*gar*) to introduce explanatory statements, see Boomershine, "Mark, the Storyteller," p. 271.

6. On the use of inside views as a way for the narrator to control distance, see Boomershine, "Mark, the Storyteller," pp. 284–314. See also Thomas E. Boomershine and Gilbert Bartholomew, "The Narrative Technique of Mark

Notes

16:8" and Boomershine, "Mark 16:8 and the Apostolic Commission," *The Journal of Biblical Literature* 100:2 (1981), 213–223 and 225–239. On distance and inside views in narrative, see Booth, *The Rhetoric of Fiction,* passim.

7. In *The Rhetoric of Fiction,* Booth shows that the implied author's beliefs and judgments are implicit in every aspect of the work, always evident to anyone who knows how to look for them (p. 20). On the relation between the narrator and the implied author, see below, note 14.

8. For examples of the complex interrelation between narrator, reader, and characters, see Petersen, " 'Point of View,' " pp. 99–101.

9. For a comprehensive treatment of the relationship between the chronological order of the events of the story and the order of events as plotted in the narrative, see Gérard Genette, *Narrative Discourse: An Essay in Method,* trans. Jane E. Lewin (Ithaca, N.Y.: Cornell University Press, 1980), especially the chapters on "Order," "Duration," and "Frequency." For a thorough discussion of this problem in Mark's story, see the essay on "Story Time and Plotted Time in Mark's Narrative" in Norman Petersen's *Literary Criticism for New Testament Critics* (Philadelphia: Fortress Press, 1978). For a discussion of suspense in narrative, see Eric Rabkin, *Narrative Suspense* (Ann Arbor: University of Michigan Press, 1973).

10. For the most comprehensive treatment of point of view in narrative, see Uspensky, *Poetics of Composition* (Berkeley: University of California Press, 1973). See also Chatman, *Story and Discourse,* pp. 151–158; Lubomir Dolezel, "The Typology of the Narrator: Point of View in Fiction," in *To Honor Roman Jacobson,* vol. 1 (The Hague: Mouton, 1967), pp. 541–552; Norman Friedman, "Point of View in Fiction: The Development of a Critical Concept," in *Approaches to the Novel,* ed. Robert Scholes (San Francisco: Chandler, 1961), pp. 113–142; J. M. Lotman, "Point of View in a Text," *New Literary History* 6 (1975): 339–352; and Robert Weimann, "Narrative Perspective: Point of View Reconsidered," in *Structure and Society in Literary History* (Charlottesville: University Press of Virginia, 1976), pp. 234–266.

11. In this way, point of view may be expressed on several planes at the same time. See Uspensky, *Poetics of Composition* and Petersen, " 'Point of View,' " pp. 13f.

12. On the two ways of thinking in Mark, see Norman Petersen's articles, especially "The Composition of Mark 4:1–8:26," *Harvard Theological Review* 73 (1980): 209ff. See also Theodore Weeden, "The Cross as Power in Weakness," in *The Passion in Mark,* ed. Werner Kelber (Philadelphia: Fortress Press, 1976), pp. 132ff.; the revealing structural analysis of Mark 15 and 16 by Daniel Patte and Aline Patte in *Structural Exegesis: From Theory to Practice* (Philadelphia: Fortress Press, 1978); and the important groundbreaking work on Mark by Dan Via, *Kerygma and Comedy in the New Testament* (Philadelphia: Fortress Press, 1975).

13. Petersen, " 'Point of View,' " pp. 101f.

14. "Standards of judgment" are most properly identified with the implied author. The "implied author" is equivalent to the "core of norms and choices" implicit in a work. This concept of the implied author is especially important in works where a "core of norms and choices" is the basis for establishing a narrator as unreliable. In a narrative like the Gospel of Mark, however, with a wholly reliable narrator, there is very little (or no) distance between the implied author and the point of view of the (reliable) narrator. The implied author is to be distinguished also from the actual author, the implied author being only the viewpoint which the actual author adopts for the organization of the narrative in a given work. On the implied author, see Booth, *The Rhetoric of Fiction*, passim, Chatman, *Story and Discourse*, pp. 147–151, and Uspensky, *Poetics of Composition*, especially p. 11.

15. See W. P. Wetherill, *The Literary Text: An Examination of Critical Methods* (Berkeley: University of California Press, 1974). Wetherill's book contains a wealth of methodological resources for dealing with style, sounds, grammar, vocabulary, meaning, rhetorical devices, and structure. For bibliography on style, see Wetherill's book. See also the many relevant articles and book reviews in the periodical *Style*.

16. On Markan style, see E. J. Pryke, *Redactional Style in the Marcan Narrative* (Cambridge: At the University Press, 1978). Boomershine discusses the rhetorical functions of many stylistic elements in "Mark, the Storyteller," passim. For an interesting and relevant discussion of the historical present in literature, see Christian Paul Casparis, *Tense Without Time: The Present Tense in Narration* (Bern: Francke Verlag, 1975).

17. We owe this suggestion to Wesley Kort.

18. Mary Ann Tolbert, "1978 Markan Seminar: Response to Robert Tannehill," presented to the Society of Biblical Literature, Markan Seminar, New Orleans, 1978 (circulated privately), pp. 3f.

19. On the repetition within episodes, see David Noble, "An Examination of the Structure in Mark's Gospel" (Ph.D. diss., University of Edinburgh, 1972). On repetition within sentence structure, see Joanna Dewey, "Markan Public Debate: Literary Technique, Concentric Structure and Theology in Mark 2:1–6," (Ph.D. diss., Graduate Theological Union, 1977, now Society of Biblical Literature Dissertation Series 48), pp. 52–54, and Boomershine, "Mark, the Storyteller," passim.

20. On verbal threads in Mark's narrative, see Boomershine, "Mark, the Storyteller," pp. 264–269. On motifs in literature, see William Freedman, "The Literary Motif: A Definition and Evaluation," *Novel* 4 (1971): 123–131.

21. For the notion of enrichment by repetition with variation, see Robert Tannehill, "The Disciples in Mark: The Function of a Narrative Role," *The Journal of Religion* 57 (1977): 396. Tannehill draws upon E. K. Brown, *Rhythm in the Novel* (Toronto: University of Toronto Press, 1950).

22. See the extensive lists in the full treatment of this narrative pattern by

Notes

Frans Neirynck, *Duality in Mark: Contributions to the Study of the Markan Redaction* (Louvain, Bel.: Louvain University Press, 1972). On the subliminal suspense related to such stylistic patterns, see Rabkin, *Narrative Suspense,* pp. 7–70.

23. For the two-fold answer to two-part questions, see David Noble, "Structure in Mark's Gospel."

24. Noted also by Boomershine, "Mark, the Storyteller."

25. See for example John Donahue, *Are You the Christ? The Trial Narrative in the Gospel of Mark,* Society of Biblical Literature Dissertation Series 10 (Missoula, Mont.: Scholars Press, 1973), pp. 58–63 and Howard Kee, *Community of the New Age: Studies in Mark's Gospel* (Philadelphia: Westminster Press, 1977), pp. 54–56. For an example of the importance of framing for interpretation, see William R. Telford, *The Barren Temple and the Withered Fig Tree* (Sheffield: JSOT, Journal for the Study of the New Testament Supplement Series I, 1980).

26. For this analysis of the concentric structure in Mark, see J. Dewey, "Markan Public Debate," and "The Literary Structure of the Controversy Stories in Mark 2:1–3:6," *Journal of Biblical Literature* 92 (1973): 394–401. See also Robert Mulholland, "The Markan Opponents of Jesus" (Ph.D. diss., Harvard University, 1977), pp. 135–174.

27. Robert Mulholland, "Opponents," p. 66.

28. Werner Kelber, "The Hour of the Son of Man and the Temptation of the Disciples (Mark 14:32–42)," in *The Passion in Mark,* pp. 52–54.

29. Alan Culpepper, "The Passion and the Resurrection in Mark," *Review and Expositor* 75 (1978): 584.

30. Norman Perrin in *Christology and a Modern Pilgrimage,* ed. Hans Dieter Betz (Society of Biblical Literature, 1971), pp. 6–10.

31. Vernon Robbins, "Summons and Outline in Mark: The Three-Step Progression," *Novum Testamentum* 23 (1981): 97–114.

32. See Tannehill, "The Disciples in Mark," pp. 398–400 and Norman Petersen, "The Composition of Mark 4:1–8:26," pp. 194–217.

33. George Nickelsburg, "The Genre and Function of the Markan Passion Narrative," *Harvard Theological Review* 73 (1980): 177f.

34. Mark also has groups of three people, such as Peter, James, and John; the elders, high priests, and legal experts; and the three women who go to the grave. For other examples, see Frans Neirynck, *Duality in Mark,* pp. 110–111.

35. For another interpretation of parables in Mark's gospel, see Madeleine Boucher, *The Mysterious Parable: A Literary Study,* Catholic Biblical Quarterly Monograph Series 6 (Washington, D.C.: Catholic Biblical Association of America, 1977). On the parables as riddles, see also Priscilla Patten, *Parable and Secret in the Gospel of Mark in Light of Select Apocryphal Literature* (Ph.D. diss., Drew University, 1976). On the function of Mark's riddles in relation to literary theory, see Frank Kermode, *The Genesis of Secrecy: On the Interpretation of Narrative* (Cambridge, Mass.:

Harvard University Press, 1979), who shows how a text both conceals and reveals, proclaims and obscures (pp. 23–47).

36. For an analysis of quotes and allusions in relation to their Old Testament background, see Howard Kee, *Community of the New Age*, pp. 45–49, and idem, "The Function of Scriptural Quotations and Allusions in Mark 11–16," in *Jesus und Paulus*, ed. E. Grässer and E. E. Ellis (Göttingen, W. Ger.: Vandenhoeck & Ruprecht, 1975), pp. 165–188. The function of these quotations in the story world needs yet to be examined.

37. Donald Juel refers to irony as the "most prominent feature of the passion story," *Messiah and Temple: The Trial of Jesus in the Gospel of Mark*, Society of Biblical Literature Dissertation Series 31 (Missoula, Mont.: Scholars Press, 1977), p. 47. On irony in the desert feedings, see Fowler ("The Feeding Stories," pp. 182–219) who has begun the only systematic treatment of irony throughout Mark by cataloging the stable commentary of the narrator upon which irony is based. ("The Feeding Stories," pp. 182–219). For irony in literature, in addition to Wayne Booth's *A Rhetoric of Irony* (Chicago: University of Chicago Press, 1974), see also D. C. Muecke, *The Compass of Irony* (London: Methuen and Co., 1970) and *Irony, The Critical Idiom* (London: Methuen and Co., 1970).

38. The false charge that Jesus will pull down the temple is false only in that it is not Jesus who will do it, but God. In this regard, note the emphatic pronoun *"I"* in the false testimony at the trial, the divine passive in Jesus' prediction of the destruction of the temple, and God's act of ripping the curtain at the point of Jesus' death.

39. For further examples of dramatic irony, see Gilbert Bilezikian, *The Liberated Gospel: A Comparison of the Gospel of Mark and Greek Tragedy* (Grand Rapids, Mich.: Baker Book House, 1977), pp. 122f.

40. See Booth, *A Rhetoric of Irony*, pp. 28–29 and Fowler, "The Feeding Stories," pp. 118–121.

3: SETTINGS

1. On settings, see Seymour Chatman, *Story and Discourse: Narrative Structure in Film and Literature* (Ithaca, N.Y.: Cornell University Press, 1978), pp. 138–145, and Robert Liddell, *A Treatise on the Novel* (London: J. Cape, 1947). For the contribution of setting to atmosphere, see Wesley Kort, *Narrative Elements and Religious Meanings* (Philadelphia: Fortress Press, 1975), pp. 20–39. Some Markan settings are relatively unimportant. We are focusing on those which contribute most to the plot.

2. For a view on the significance of Passover for Mark's gospel, see John Bowman, *The Gospel of Mark: The New Christian Jewish Passover Haggadah* (Leiden, Neth.: E. J. Brill, 1965).

3. Concerning the "way" motif, see Werner Kelber, *Mark's Story of Jesus* (Philadelphia: Fortress Press, 1978). Kelber has dealt extensively with many Markan settings in *The Kingdom in Mark: A New Place and a New Time*

(Philadelphia: Fortress Press, 1974). See also Joanna Dewey, *Disciples of the Way: Mark on Discipleship* (Women's Division, Board of Global Ministries, United Methodist Church, 1976) as well as Willard Swartley, *Mark: The Way for All Nations* (Scotsdale, Ariz.: Herald Press, 1979), and idem, "The Structural Function of the 'Way' (*Hodos*) in Mark's Gospel," in *The New Way of Jesus*, ed. William Klassen (Kansas: Faith and Life Press, 1980), pp. 73–86.

4. See Norman Perrin, "Towards an Interpretation of the Gospel of Mark," in *Christology and a Modern Pilgrimage*, ed. Hans D. Betz (Society of Biblical Literature, 1971), pp. 7–30.

5. For the background of many of these settings in Israel's history, see Willard Swartley, "A Study of Markan Structure: The Influence of Holy History upon the Structure of the Gospel of Mark," (Ph.D. diss., Princeton Theological Seminary, 1973). See also Ulrich Mauser, *Christ in the Wilderness* (London: SCM Press, 1963).

6. On Mark's use of two desert feedings to emphasize the lack of faith among the disciples, see Robert Fowler, "The Feeding Stories in the Gospel of Mark," (Ph.D. diss., University of Chicago, 1978).

7. Several of these settings also recall events associated with Biblical narratives about the prophets Elijah and Elisha. For Markan parallels to these narratives, see the forthcoming work of Wolfgang Roth.

8. Kelber views the sea as a stormy passage from Jewish to gentile territory (*The Kingdom in Mark*, pp. 45–65). For a differing view, see Fowler, "Feeding Stories," pp. 70–82.

9. Robert Tannehill, "The Disciples in Mark: The Function of a Narrative Role," *Journal of Religion* 57 (1977): 398–400.

10. We owe this suggestion to Wesley Kort.

11. On the significance of the Temple in Mark, see especially Donald Juel, *Messiah and Temple: The Trial of Jesus in the Gospel of Mark*, Society of Biblical Literature Dissertation Series 31 (Missoula, Mont.: Scholar's Press, 1977).

12. First suggested to us by Vernon Robbins. On the significance of Galilee, see also Kelber, *The Kingdom in Mark*, pp. 129–147.

4: THE PLOT

1. On conflict analysis in relation to plot, see Lawrence Perrine, *Story and Structure* (New York: Harcourt, Brace and World, 1966), pp. 48–65. Conflict contributes not only to the structure of the plot but also may set the tone, define characters, and determine atmosphere in a narrative. In addition to general works on narrative which treat plot, see also Norman Friedman, "Forms of the Plot," in *The Theory of the Novel*, ed. Philip Stevick (New York: Free Press, 1967), pp. 145–166, and Kieran Egan, "What is a Plot?" *New Literary History* 9 (1978): 455–474.

2. For other depictions of the larger cosmic framework of the story, see

James M. Robinson, *The Problem of History in Mark and Other Marcan Studies* (Philadelphia: Fortress Press, 1982); Ernest Best, *The Temptation and the Passion: The Markan Soteriology* (Cambridge: At the University Press, 1965); James Wilde, "A Social Description of the Community Reflected in the Gospel of Mark" (Ph.D. diss., Drew University, 1974); and Werner Kelber, *The Kingdom in Mark: A New Place and a New Time* (Philadelphia: Fortress Press, 1974).

3. On God's role in the story, see John Donahue, "A Neglected Factor in the Theology of Mark" (Society of Biblical Literature Paper in the Markan Seminar, 1980).

4. The analogy of Jesus as commissioned agent of God is important for Mark, especially in the riddle of the vineyard. On commissioned agents in the ancient world, see Peder Borgen, "God's Agent in the Fourth Gospel," in *Religions in Antiquity,* ed. J. Neusner (Leiden, Neth.: E. J. Brill, 1968), pp. 137–148.

5. There is extensive literature on the secrecy and hiddenness motifs in Mark. For a careful sorting out of various aspects of these motifs, see Eugene Lemcio, "Some New Proposals for Interpreting the Gospel of Mark" (Ph.D. diss., University of Cambridge, 1974).

6. On exorcisms, see Best, *The Temptation and the Passion;* David Bartlett, "Exorcism Stories in the Gospel of Mark" (Ph.D. diss., Yale University, 1972); and Robinson, *The Problem of History in Mark.*

7. See David Rhoads, *Israel in Revolution 6–74 C.E.* (Philadelphia: Fortress Press, 1976).

8. On blasphemy, see Donald Juel, *Messiah and Temple: The Trial of Jesus in the Gospel of Mark,* Society of Biblical Literature Dissertation Series 31 (Missoula, Mont.: Scholars Press, 1977), p. 103. In this story, blasphemy is a violation of God either for taking on the prerogatives of God (of which the authorities accuse Jesus) or as a vicious, even though unknowing, attack on God or his agent (of which Jesus accuses the authorities).

9. The parallel position in the concentric structure of the five conflict stories reinforces the notion that the sabbath offense in the last episode was as serious as a charge of blasphemy in the first episode. See also Joanna Dewey, "Markan Public Debate: Literary Technique, Rhetorical Structure and Theology in Mark 2:1–6" (Ph.D. diss., Graduate Theological Union, 1977).

10. On toll collectors and sinners, see John R. Donahue, "Tax Collectors and Sinners," *Catholic Biblical Quarterly* 33 (1979): 139–61.

11. The authorities appear to treat the statement itself as blasphemy. Eugene Lemcio has suggested in private conversation that perhaps the statement is considered blasphemous in the story world because it is uttered by this particular man; that is, the authorities considered it blasphemous that Jesus—who had done such offensive actions, such as cleansing the temple and healing on the Sabbath—should claim his authority is from God.

Notes

12. See J. Dewey, "Markan Public Debate," pp. 122, 137, 188.

13. For a full depiction of these patterns, see J. Dewey, "Markan Public Debate," pp. 114–192, 210–211.

14. See the progressive patterns showing the lessening of opposition in the seven conflict stories in Jerusalem, in J. Dewey, "Markan Public Debate," pp. 271–290.

15. Thomas E. Boomershine, "Mark, the Storyteller: A Rhetorical-Critical Investigation of Mark's Passion and Resurrection Narrative" (Ph.D. diss., Union Theological Seminary, New York, 1974), p. 180.

16. On the trial of Jesus in Mark, see J. Donahue, *Are You the Christ? The Trial Narrative in the Gospel of Mark,* Society of Biblical Literature Dissertation Series 10 (Missoula, Mont.: Scholars Press, 1973).

17. See Robert Tannehill, "The Gospel of Mark as Narrative Christology," *Semeia* 16 (1979): 78–79.

18. At the crucifixion, the narrator describes the high priests' ridicule of Jesus as blasphemy.

19. See Tannehill, "Narrative Christology."

20. See J. Dewey, *Disciples of the Way: Mark on Discipleship* (Women's Division, Board of Global Ministries, United Methodist Church, 1976).

21. See Boomershine, "Mark, the Storyteller," pp. 130, 135–142.

22. See Robert Fowler, "The Feeding Stories in the Gospel of Mark" (Ph.D. diss., University of Chicago, 1978), pp. 112–181.

23. On this third boat scene, see Tannehill, "The Disciples in Mark: The Function of a Narrative Role," *Journal of Religion* 57 (1977): 386–405 and Norman Petersen, "The Composition of Mark 4:1–8:26," *Harvard Theological Review* 73:1–2 (1980): 185–217.

24. On Jesus' preparation for his absence, see Kelber, *The Kingdom in Mark,* pp. 109ff.

25. Boomershine, "Mark, the Storyteller," pp. 150–154.

26. See J. Dewey, "Mark 10:35–40 from the Perspective of the Implied Reader: The Disciples as a Narrative Device," (Society of Biblical Literature Paper in the Markan Seminar, 1979).

27. For various conclusions about the fate of the disciples in relation to the ending, see T. J. Weeden, *Mark—Traditions in Conflict* (Philadelphia: Fortress Press, 1971); Werner Kelber, *Mark's Story of Jesus* (Philadelphia: Fortress Press, 1978); Tannehill, "The Disciples in Mark"; idem, "Narrative Christology"; Boomershine, "Mark, the Storyteller"; J. Dewey, *Disciples of the Way;* idem, "Implied Reader"; N. Petersen, "When is an End not the End?" *Interpretation* 34 (1980): 151–166; Kim Dewey, "Peter's Curse and Cursed Peter," in *The Passion in Mark,* ed. Werner Kelber (Philadelphia: Fortress Press, 1976), pp. 96–114; among others.

28. The "rooster crow" may refer to the bugle sound which ends the night watch. See K. Dewey, "Peter's Curse and Cursed Peter" in *The Passion in Mark,* p. 102.

29. Mary Ann Tolbert, "1978 Markan Seminar: Response to Robert

Tannehill," presented to the Society of Biblical Literature, Markan Seminar, New Orleans, 1978 (circulated privately), pp. 7f.

30. See James Robinson, *The Problem of History in Mark,* pp. 43–46.

31. We are indebted to Wesley Kort for this insight.

5: THE CHARACTERS

1. On character, see especially Seymour Chatman, *Story and Discourse: Narrative Structure in Fiction and Film* (Ithaca, N.Y.: Cornell University Press, 1978), pp. 107–138; W. J. Harvey, *Character and the Novel* (Ithaca, N.Y.: Cornell University Press, 1966); and the chapter on character in Robert Scholes and Robert Kellogg, *The Nature of Narrative* (New York: Oxford University Press, 1966), pp. 160–206. Theodore Weeden initiated the study of character in Mark's gospel in *Mark—Traditions in Conflict* (Philadelphia: Fortress Press, 1971).

2. This is the focus of the stimulating analysis of Markan characters by Robert Tannehill, "The Gospel of Mark as Narrative Christology," *Semeia* 16 (1979): 57–92. See also his "The Disciples in Mark: The Function of a Narrative Role," *Journal of Religion* 57 (1977): 386–405.

3. See Chatman, *Story,* pp. 107–138.

4. The various Jewish groups can be characterized independently, but in terms of their function in the plot the differences are minor. Our concern here is with the coordinate function of these groups in the ongoing conflict with Jesus. Note also how the legal experts, or scribes, provide a unifying connection with all the groups of authorities. See Michael J. Cook, *Mark's Treatment of the Jewish Leaders,* Supplements to *Novum Testamentum* (Leiden, Neth.: E. J. Brill, 1979) and Robert Mulholland, "The Markan Opponents of Jesus" (Ph.D. diss., Harvard University, 1977), pp. 131–134.

5. Tannehill, "Narrative Christology," p. 67.

6. For a literary treatment of John the Baptist, see Ronald Kittel, "John the Baptist in the Gospel According to Mark" (Ph.D. diss., Graduate Theological Union, 1977).

7. On "showing" and "telling," see Wayne Booth, *The Rhetoric of Fiction* (Chicago: University of Chicago Press, 1961), pp. 3–16.

8. On the use of standards of judgment in relation to character, see Thomas E. Boomershine, "Mark, the Storyteller: A Rhetorical-Critical Investigation of Mark's Passion and Resurrection Narrative" (Ph.D. diss., Union Theological Seminary, New York, 1974), pp. 276–284; and Tannehill, "Narrative Christology," pp. 62, 73.

9. On distance in narrative, see Booth, *The Rhetoric of Fiction,* pp. 243–271. On Mark's gospel, see Boomershine, "Mark, the Storyteller," pp. 284–314.

10. Boris Uspensky notes that the motives of a character's behavior are often revealed by the context and situation rather than by a depiction of the

Notes

character's inner thoughts or feelings, *Poetics of Composition: The Structure of the Artistic Text and Typology of a Compositional Form,* trans. Valentina Zavarin and Susan Wittig (Berkeley: University of California Press, 1973), pp. 121ff.

11. In his discussion of traits, Chatman draws upon work by psychologists. See especially Gordon Allport, "What is a Trait of Personality?" *Journal of Abnormal and Social Psychology* 25 (1931): 368 and *Trait-Names: A Psycho-lexical Study,* with Henry Odbert, *Psychological Monographs,* vol. 47 (Princeton: Psychological Review Co., 1936).

12. These categories were suggested by E. M. Forster, *Aspects of the Novel* (New York: Harcourt, Brace and World, 1927), pp. 65–82.

13. For an analysis of this reading process, see Wolfgang Iser, *The Implied Reader: Patterns of Communication in Prose Fiction from Bunyan to Beckett* (Baltimore: Johns Hopkins University Press, 1974), pp. 274–294 and idem, *The Act of Reading: A Theory of Aesthetic Response* (Baltimore: Johns Hopkins University Press, 1978).

14. On the character study of Jesus, see especially Tannehill, "Narrative Christology," passim.

15. On the notion of uncleanness in relation to Mark's gospel, see Marla Schierling, "Woman, Cult, and Miracle Recital: Mark 5:24–34" (Ph.D. diss., St. Louis University, 1980).

16. Certain elements of the text support the notion that the narrator characterizes Jesus as one who discovers his limitations and his mission in the course of his activity.

17. See Robert Mulholland, "The Markan Opponents of Jesus," (Ph.D. diss., Harvard University, 1977).

18. See Norman Perrin, "The High Priest's Question and Jesus' Answer," in *The Passion in Mark,* ed. Werner Kelber (Philadelphia: Fortress Press, 1976), pp. 81ff.

19. See especially Joanna Dewey, *Disciples of the Way: Mark on Discipleship* (Women's Division, Board of Global Ministries, United Methodist Church, 1976) pp. 99ff.

20. On the ways Jesus serves in healing, see especially J. Dewey, *Disciples of the Way,* pp. 101–104.

21. On the many aspects of Jesus as teacher, see Vernon Robbins, "The Genre of Mark: Expectation and Adaptation" (unpublished manuscript); Allan Howe, "The Teaching Jesus Figure in the Gospel of Mark: A Redaction-Critical Study in Markan Christology" (Ph.D. diss., Northwestern University, 1978); and Robert Meye, *Jesus and the Twelve* (Grand Rapids, Mich.: Wm. B. Eerdmans, 1968), pp. 30–87.

22. See J. Dewey, *Disciples of the Way,* p. 102.

23. On the significance of the fig tree episode in relation to the temple cleansing, see William Telford, "The Barren Temple and the Withered Fig Tree," (Ph.D. diss., Cambridge University, 1976).

24. When Jesus does not tell people to be quiet, as with the demoniac who had the Legion, he is threatened neither by an indictment nor by a large crowd.

25. See David Aune, "The Problem of the Messianic Secret," *Novum Testamentum* 11 (1969): 31.

26. When the disciples think he is a ghost walking on the sea, Jesus says "I am" (It is I), and when the High Priest asks whether he is the anointed one, he answers "I am" (Yes, I am).

27. There is extensive literature on the Markan use of the "son of man" traditions in light of Jewish literature. See, for example, Norman Perrin, *A Modern Pilgrimage in New Testament Christology* (Philadelphia: Fortress Press, 1974), especially pp. 84–94.

28. For this notion of enticement to false hopes, see Boomershine, "Mark, the Storyteller," pp. 318–327, followed by Tannehill, "Narrative Christology," pp. 85–87.

29. The precise meaning of "ransom" is not clear. It seems best to relate it in general to the notion of covenant. It may also be related to the lamb sacrificed at Passover, which signified the means by which the angel of death passed over the Israelites.

30. See John Dominic Crossan, "A Form for Absence: The Markan Creation of Gospel," *Semeia* 12 (1978): 41–55.

31. In Mark's story, Jesus' death is not connected with forgiveness of sins. Pardon is already secured by John's baptism and Jesus' authority. See also Culpepper, "Passion," p. 587.

32. On the authorities, see especially Tannehill, "Narrative Christology"; Boomershine, "Mark, the Storyteller," passim; J. Dewey, "Markan Public Debate: Literary Technique, Concentric Structure and Theology in Mark 2:1–3:6" (Ph.D. diss., Graduate Theological Union, 1977); and Mulholland, "The Markan Opponents."

33. In the narrative world, what keeps the wise legal expert from being *in* the rule of God is that the legal experts consider the anointed one a son of David rather than David's lord. See R. Mulholland, "Opponents" (Ph.D. diss., Harvard University, 1977), pp. 118ff.

34. See especially J. Dewey's analysis of the seven conflict stories in Galilee in "Markan Public Debate," pp. 271–290.

35. On the illegalities of the trial, see John Donahue, *Are You the Christ? The Trial Narrative in the Gospel of Mark,* Society of Biblical Literature Dissertation Series 10 (Missoula, Mont.: Scholars Press, 1973) and Donald Juel, *Messiah and Temple: The Trial of Jesus in the Gospel of Mark,* Society of Biblical Literature Dissertation Series 31 (Missoula, Mont.: Scholars Press, 1977), p. 59.

36. The worst of the legal experts "eat up the houses of the widows." On the mentality of the authorities, see Anitra Kolenkow, "Beyond Miracles, Suffering, and Eschatology," *Society of Biblical Literature Seminar Papers,*

vol. 2, ed. George MacRae (Missoula, Mont.: Scholars Press, 1973) and J. Dewey, *Disciples of the Way*, pp. 105ff.

37. On the extensive parallels between the execution of John by Herod and the execution of Jesus by Pilate, see Kittel, "John the Baptist," pp. 102–113 and Boomershine, "Mark, the Storyteller," pp. 306ff.

38. On distance in relation to the disciples, see Boomershine, "Mark, the Storyteller," pp. 308–314.

39. See Tannehill, "The Disciples in Mark," pp. 396–405.

40. On development in the disciples, see J. Dewey, *Disciples of the Way*, passim, and Weeden, *Mark*, pp. 26–51.

41. See Joseph Tyson, "The Blindness of the Disciples in Mark," *Journal of Biblical Literature* 80 (1961): 261–268 and David J. Hawkin, "The Incomprehension of the Disciples," *Journal of Biblical Literature* 91 (1972): 491–500, among others.

42. Tannehill, "The Disciples in Mark," pp. 398ff.

43. Harry Daniel, "The Transfiguration (Mark 9:2–13 and Parallels)" (Ph.D. diss., Vanderbilt University, 1976), pp. 63–64.

44. See the excellent discussion in J. Dewey, *Disciples of the Way*, pp. 72–120.

45. See Boomershine, "Mark the Storyteller," p. 141.

46. The brief episode about the arrest and flight of a naked young man reinforces the shame of the disciples' flight and foreshadows the real threat to Peter in the following scenes. See Harry Fleddermann, "The Flight of the Naked Young Man (Mark 14:51–52)," *Catholic Biblical Quarterly* 41 (1979): 412–418.

47. On the "anxious self-concern" of the disciples, see Tannehill, "The Disciples in Mark," pp. 400ff. and idem, *Mirror for the Disciples* (Nashville: Discipleship Resources, 1977).

48. For this analysis, see especially Boomershine, "Mark 16:8 and the Apostolic Commission," *Journal of Biblical Literature*, 100:2 (1981): 225–239, and idem, "Mark, the Storyteller," pp. 138ff., 154, 169, 308–314. See also J. Dewey, "Mark 10:35–40 from the Perspective of the Implied Reader: The Disciples as a Narrative Device" (Society of Biblical Literature, Markan Seminar Paper, 1979).

49. On these minor characters, see especially J. Dewey, *Disciples of the Way* and Tannehill, "Narrative Christology," p. 63.

50. On the role of women in Mark's Gospel, see J. Dewey, *Disciples of the Way*, pp. 123–134, and Schierling, "Woman, Cult, and Miracle Recital," passim.

51. See Tannehill, "Narrative Christology," p. 67.

52. See also Eduard Schweizer, "The Portrayal of the Life of Faith in the Gospel of Mark," *Interpretation* 32 (1978): 395ff.

53. See Schierling, "Woman, Cult, and Miracle Recital," passim.

54 J. Dewey, *Disciples of the Way*, pp. 104ff.

55. See Tannehill, "The Disciples in Mark," pp. 404ff.
56. We owe this suggestion to J. Dewey.
57. On the crowds, see also Rebecca Patten, "The Thaumaturgical Element in the Gospel of Mark," (Ph.D. diss., Drew University, 1976).

CONCLUSION

1. Robert Scholes defines the implied reader as a "property of the text itself, each text implying a particular ideal reader, equipped with certain kinds of knowledge and experience, and capable of being manipulated in certain ways." See "Cognition and the Implied Reader," *Diacritics* 5 (1975): 14. Robert Crossman defines the implied reader as "the image in the literary text of the reader as the [implied] author desires him." See "In Defense of Authors and Readers," *Novel* 11 (1977): 5–25. See also Wayne Booth, *The Rhetoric of Fiction* (Chicago: University of Chicago Press, 1961), passim; Seymour Chatman, *Story and Discourse: Narrative Structure in Fiction and Film* (Ithaca, N.Y.: Cornell University Press, 1978), pp. 147–151; Gerald Prince, "Notes Towards a Categorization of Fictional Narratees," *Genre* 4 (1971): 100–105; and Walter Ong, "The Writer's Audience is Always a Fiction," *Interfaces of the Word* (Ithaca, N.Y.: Cornell University Press, 1977).
2. Among Markan scholars, Mary Ann Tolbert argues that the ideal reader aligns with Jesus and is betrayed by the disciples who fail Jesus, in "Response to Robert Tannehill" (Society of Biblical Literature, Markan Seminar Paper, 1978); Joanna Dewey agrees that the ideal reader aligns with Jesus, but that the reader retains interest in the fate of the disciples, in "Mark 10:35–40 from the Perspective of the Implied Reader: The Disciples as a Narrative Device" (Society of Biblical Literature, Markan Seminar Paper, 1979); and Robert Tannehill argues that "the reader identifies at first with the disciples but then rejects them and identifies with Jesus" in "The Disciples in Mark: The Function of a Narrative Role," *Journal of Religion* 57 (1977): 386–405. Tannehill works with the concept of the implied reader developed by Wolfgang Iser, *The Implied Reader: Patterns of Communication in Prose Fiction from Bunyan to Beckett* (Baltimore: Johns Hopkins University Press, 1974) and idem, *The Act of Reading: A Theory of Aesthetic Response* (Baltimore: Johns Hopkins University Press, 1978). Identification or alignment with characters is a complex matter. See, for example, Hans Robert Jones, "Levels of Identification of Hero and Audience," *New Literary History* 5 (1974): 283–317.
3. And there are many ways of interpreting the story. On multiplicity in interpretation, see Booth's *Critical Interpretation: The Powers and Limits of Pluralism* (Chicago: University of Chicago Press, 1979). On biblical interpretation, see Mary Ann Tolbert, *Perspectives on the Parables: An Approach to Multiple Interpretations* (Philadelphia: Fortress Press, 1979). On the indeterminacy and open-endedness of the text, see Frank Kermode,

Notes

The Genesis of Secrecy: On the Interpretation of Narrative (Cambridge, Mass.: Harvard University Press, 1979).

4. This whole idea of the narrative making of the reader a faithful disciple was first presented and developed by Tolbert, "Response to Robert Tannehill."

5. The actual reader in contrast to the implied reader is aware not only of the story world but also of the real world. We are indebted to J. Dewey for this suggestion.

6. For an analysis of the Roman-Jewish War, see David Rhoads, *Israel in Revolution 6–74 C.E.* (Philadelphia: Fortress Press, 1976).

7. On these points see Werner Kelber, *The Kingdom in Mark: A New Place and a New Time* (Philadelphia: Fortress Press, 1974). See also Lloyd Gaston, *No Stone on Another: Studies in the Significance of the Fall of Jerusalem in the Synoptic Gospels* (Leiden, Neth.: E. J. Brill, 1970).

8. In recent decades, the focus of much literary interpretation has shifted from the text to the reader. See Vincent Leitch, "A Primer of Recent Critical Theories," *College English* 39 (1977): 138–152 and Steven Mailloux, "Reader Response Criticism?" *Genre* (1977): 413–431. Discussions of the readers of Mark's gospel will be aided by clear distinctions between the implied reader as ideal reader, the implied reader of Iser's model, a hypothetical historical reader of the first century, and an actual reader whose responses are valued without regard to the appropriate responses implied by the narrative.

9. We are indebted to J. Dewey for this suggestion.

10. In addition to the books cited throughout, we have found the following works helpful for teaching literary analysis: William C. Dowling, *The Critic's Hornbook* (New York: Thomas Y. Crowell, 1977); Karen Hess, *Appreciating Literature, A Self-Teaching Guide* (New York: John Wiley and Sons, 1978); and Laurence Perrine, *Story and Structure* (New York: Harcourt, Brace, and World, 1966). For a fascinating collection of contemporary short stories on themes which parallel the Gospel of Mark, see John O'Brien and Richard Finholt, eds., *No Signs from Heaven* (New York: Dell, 1975). See also our "Study Guide on the Gospel of Mark as Story" (prepared and circulated privately under a grant from the Siebert Lutheran Foundation, 1978), which contains exercises and questions for use in exploring the literary features of Mark's gospel. For literary criticism in relation to the New Testament, see also William Beardslee, *Literary Criticism of the New Testament* (Philadelphia: Fortress Press, 1970); Norman Petersen, *Literary Criticism for New Testament Critics* (Philadelphia: Fortress Press, 1978); and the works of Amos Wilder, especially *Early Christian Rhetoric* (Cambridge, Mass.: Harvard University Press, 1971).